The Australian Horn of Plenty

Hamilton explores in a short history how all men gained the vote, self-government and the secret ballot in South Australia (1856), Victoria (1857), and New South Wales (1858).

Australia permanently democratised without a violent revolution, and at a very early time. In 1851–1858, local parliaments in the British colonies of New South Wales, Victoria, and South Australia drafted laws which gave all men the vote, including Aboriginal and Chinese men, the secret ballot, and self-government of local affairs. Britain approved, this book examines the parliamentary debates which led to these radical democracies. Debates covered voting eligibility, the secret ballot, the upper house of parliament, equal electorates, multiple voting, illiterate voters, control of Crown lands, terms of parliament, payment of members, and separation of Church and State. British parliamentary tradition was combined with the advanced liberal thinking of the time, Chartism with the British constitution. The democratisation of 1851–1858 in the three largest Australian colonies was as fundamental to Australian prosperity as the 'mixed' market economy.

This is a vital text for scholars of democracy as well as those interested in Australian Studies, Australian History, Political Science, Constitutional Law, and the building blocks of first-world prosperity.

Reg Hamilton is Adjunct Professor, Central Queensland University, College of Business, School of Business and Law, formerly a Deputy President of the Fair Work Commission and Australian Industrial Relations Commission. He is the author of numerous articles on the history of the minimum wage, and books on labour relations and Australian colonial history.

The Australian Horn
of Plenty

How Britain's Australian Colonies
Began Democracy

Reg Hamilton

Routledge
Taylor & Francis Group

LONDON AND NEW YORK

First published 2024
by Routledge
4 Park Square, Milton Park, Abingdon, Oxon, OX14 4RN

and by Routledge
605 Third Avenue, New York, NY 10158

Routledge is an imprint of the Taylor & Francis Group, an informa business

© 2024 Reg Hamilton

British Library Cataloguing-in-Publication Data
A catalogue record for this book is available from the British Library

ISBN: 9781032791449 (hbk)
ISBN: 9781032791463 (pbk)
ISBN: 9781003490739 (ebk)

DOI: 10.4324/9781003490739

Typeset in Times New Roman
by KnowledgeWorks Global Ltd.

Contents

Previous publication

Some of the material in this document is drawn from R Hamilton, *Colony: Strange Origins of One of the Earliest Modern Democracies*, Wakefield Press, SA, 2010.

I acknowledge comments on an earlier version of this history by Frank Bongiorno, Professor of History, Australian National University, and Sean Scalmer, Professor of Australian History, University of Melbourne. However, the responsibility for its contents is mine. I acknowledge the comments of anonymous referees. I acknowledge Tricia Curry, images.

I am indebted to those who hold and organise the records of this early history such as the State Library of South Australia, the other State libraries, and the national 'documenting democracy' resources.

Aboriginal and Torres Strait Islander people should be aware that this book contains names and words of people now deceased.

Introduction

My 40-year career concerned the standard of living of workers and the need for a more productive economy.[1] I became interested in how such comparative prosperity for ordinary people developed in Australia.

Part of the answer is that it began in the 1850s with radical constitutions and electoral laws which gave all men self-government, the vote, and secret ballot in three Australian colonies. The new laws required parliaments to address the needs of voters.

The 1850s debates which led to these laws are the subject of this book and are not well covered in many historical accounts. There is no one record of them available; this book is an attempt to fill the gap using the limited records available.

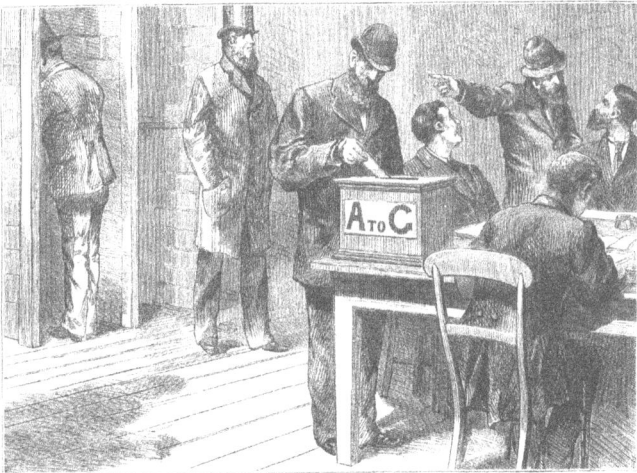

Figure 0.1 Interior of a polling booth

DOI: 10.4324/9781003490739-1

The result of Australian governance which came from democratisation is that Australia now does exceptionally well measured by the UN Human Development Index for example and all similar measures.[2] These are measurable 'facts on the ground.' The market economy was developed. Australia 'rode on the sheep's back' and ordinary people became prosperous, helped by a legislated 'safety net' of democracy, health, education, welfare, progressive taxation, and labour laws which was gradually developed.[3] Australia was an early and successful proponent of the modern 'mixed' economy of ameliorative liberalism which addressed needs of those left behind and introduced a common citizenship.[4]

In 2024 more than half of the world's population (over 4 billion people) will have elections, and of 71 elections only 43 will have fully free and fair votes.[5]

It seems as odd and anomalous as the platypus that elections held under the democratic 1850s constitutions could today be classified as a 'flawed democracy'[6] such as the United States, but not presumably 'fully free and fair votes,'[7] except for the exclusion of women.

So well did the 1850s parliamentarians do their job that parliament resolved a difficult political debate and gave votes to women in South Australia in 1895 with a simple two-page amendment.[8]

Figure 0.2 Catherine Helen Spence, led campaigns for votes for women – Preface, p. 2

Notes

1 For 17 years I worked for the Australian Chamber of Commerce and Industry (and predecessors) (1984–2001) ending as Manager, Labour Relations. I then spent 21 years as a Deputy President of the Fair Work Commission (and predecessors) (2001–2022). During the Hawke/Keating and Howard Governments (1984–2001), I was an employer representative on the NLCC Committee on Industrial Legislation, which reviewed and developed draft legislation. The focus of the national debates on labour legislation for employers was a productive economy, as well as equity. I represented employers as advocate in the test cases 1991–2001 in the Australian Industrial Relations Commission, including nine test cases on adjusting the minimum wage. In Australia industrial tribunals, not Government, fix the minimum wage.
2 For example, Australia performs exceptionally well on the UN Human Development Index (HDI), at 0.951, compared to Norway at 0.961 and the United States at 0.921 in 2023. The HDI is a summary measure of the following things: **Health:** life expectancy at birth; **Knowledge:** mean years of schooling for adults aged 25 years and above and expected years of schooling for children; **Standard of Living:** GNI Per Capita; https://hdr.undp.org/data-center/human-development-index#/indicies/ HDI; accessed December 2023; M Read, 'Australians are the world's richest people,' Australian Financial Review, 20 September 2022. https://www.afr.com/policy/ economy/australians-are-the-world-s-richest-people-20220920-p5bjg4
3 See, e.g., Isaac J., and Macintyre S., *The New Province for Law and Order* (Cambridge University Press, 2004); R. Hamilton, *Colony: Strange Origins of One of the Earliest Modern Democracies* (SA: Wakefield Press, 2010), 9; R. Hamilton, *Waltzing Matilda and the Sunshine Harvester Factory* (Fair Work Commission, 2010); I.W. McLean, *Why Australia Prospered: The Shifting Sources of Economic Growth* (NJ: Princeton University Press, 2013); and B. Dickey, *No Charity There: A Short History of Social Welfare in Australia* (London: Routledge, 1987).
4 Using the term not as a mix of the free market with socialism but as adding a legislated safety net to the market economy to protect those left behind, the vulnerable and poor, or to establish a common citizenship.
5 According to The Economist, 13 November 2023, '2024 is the biggest election year in history,' economist.com.
6 'Elections are free, fair and allow for the possibility of change, but their political systems have weaknesses.'
7 The Economist, '2024 is the biggest election year in history,' 13 November 2023, economist.com.
8 Constitution (Female Suffrage) Act 1895 (SA). It also gave women the right to stand for parliament, the first in the world.

Bibliography

Constitution (Female Suffrage) Act 1895 (SA).
Dickey, Brian. *No charity There: A Short History of Social Welfare in Australia.* London: Routledge, 1987.
Hamilton, Reg. *Colony: Strange Origins of One of the Earliest Modern Democracies.* Kent Town, South Australia, Wakefield Press,, 2010, 9.
Hamilton, Reg. *Waltzing Matilda and the Sunshine Harvester Factory.* Melbourne, Fair Work Commission, 2010.

Isaac, Joseph, and Stuart Macintyre. *The New Province for Law and Order*. Sydney, Cambridge University Press, 2004.

McLean, Ian.W. *Why Australia Prospered: The Shifting Sources of Economic Growth*. NJ: Princeton University Press, 2013.

Read, M, 'Australians are the world's richest people', Australian Financial Review, 20 September 2022. https://www.afr.com/policy/economy/australians-are-the-world-s-richest-people-20220920-p5bjg4

The Economist, '2024 is the biggest election year in history,' 13 November 2023, economist.com

The UN Human Development Index (HDI) https://hdr.undp.org/data-center/human-development-index#/indicies/HDI; accessed December 2023.

1 Democracy

Abstract

While nearly all first-world nations are democracies, the constitutional arrangements and voting systems vary. Nevertheless, key elements such as free elections to the legislatures and free speech are necessary. Parliaments responsive to the popular will are the result, which therefore address issues of poverty or the standard of living of ordinary people that voters require. Governments are judged, often harshly, and dismissed from office. Wider ideals such as freedom and equality mean that all democratic systems are 'approaching democracy' rather than simply implementing it, because of the wide scope for argument about how to apply such ideals.

Definitions

The modern liberal democracies that operate in Australia today are not identical to those in other industrialised, first-world nations. However, each democracy provides for self-government through parliaments and elected officials, elected by a democratic procedure using 'one person one vote,' accompanied by the rule of law and guarantees of free speech, and freedom to vote.

Governments are often judged harshly by the electorate and dismissed from office. Democracy is a humbling experience for political leaders.

It resembles natural justice, the right of those affected to have their say in court or before actions are taken by government to their detriment, first established by a British court decision in 1863 in *Cooper v Wandsworth Board of Works*.[1]

Free debate in which facts are made widely known and debated helps good government. As John Stuart Mill said, if a proposition 'is not fully, frequently, and fearlessly discussed, it will be held as a dead dogma, not a living truth.'[2]

One constitutional lawyer described the development of the radical Australian democracies as 'the harmonizing of the executive with the legislature,' then 'the harmonizing of the legislature with popular opinion.'[3]

DOI: 10.4324/9781003490739-2

A NORTH BOURKE CANDIDATE ADDRESSING HIS CONSTITUENCY ON A "NATIONAL" QUESTION

Figure 1.1 A North Bourke candidate addressing his constituency on a 'national' question

Ivor Jennings said,

> Democracy, as we understand it, means that the people must be free, the free choose the rulers, and the rulers govern according to the wishes of the people.[4]

Boyle Travers Finniss, the first Premier under responsible Government in South Australia, said that the Real Property Act 1857 (Torrens title) was 'strictly forced upon the Governor and Parliament by the will of the people … few members dared to vote against any of its provisions.'[5] Torrens title was together with Alfred Deakin's wages boards of 1896 possibly the most influential Australian colonial Act world-wide apart from democracy and the secret ballot.

The results of democracy

What does democracy mean for the standard of living and circumstances of ordinary people? The Chartist leader Joseph Rayner Stephens said in 1838 that voting rights were a 'knife and fork, a bread and cheese question.'[6]

Boyle Travers Finniss said local adoption of 'the advanced liberal principles in the mother country,' meant that 'no man can gain or hold power' unless 'he not only professes but acts in the full determination to use his influence and his power to promote the general advance of the community in wealth by such measures as shall tend to its distribution, not amongst any particular class but amongst those who have raised him to power by their votes, and who, under the present political and commercial systems, are not receiving their just share of the increasing wealth of the State.'[7]

Democracy is a means of obtaining good government to address for example economic difficulties or poverty. It is also a means for men and women to have a say in Government and influence it. It is an end in itself.

Popular opinion in the colonies required land reform to give ordinary people more access to land in what was mainly an agricultural and pastoral economy, just as the Chartists had a land reform programme. After democratic self-government was achieved in the 1850s, land reform became a bitter political issue for the rest of the century in the Australian colonies. Partly successful land reform legislation was enacted over the opposition of the squatters. Australia 'rode on the sheep's back' for over a hundred years.

Constitutional arrangements and voting systems

There are a wide range of constitutional arrangements. First-world democracies include constitutional monarchies, republics, elected presidents, Westminster systems in which the executive is answerable to the lower house of parliament, and hybrids of these.

Nearly all 'first world' countries are democracies. Millions more refugees and economic migrants would move to first-world countries if only they could, to benefit from their prosperity and good governance. There may be some form of modern consensus that the first-world liberal democracies are comparatively well governed – even the best governed – and the most prosperous for ordinary people.

After self-government 'first past the post' voting was used in the three colonies, as in Britain today, in which one vote is cast by each voter and the candidate with the most votes wins. There are many voting systems now used in first-world countries, from preferential voting in which more than one vote is cast and second and third and more preferences are distributed until a majority is reached, to proportional representation, in which winners are based on proportions of total votes cast.

One commentator sees the British empire, within which these radical colonial experiments occurred, as a 'midwife' of new democratic institutions despite the tension between an empire and representative democracy in which power relations are 'contingent … permanently in need of public checking and humbling through such mechanisms as periodic elections ….'[8]

Conclusion

There are wider ideals such as freedom, equality, order, stability, majority rule, protection of minority rights, and participation. Any system can only be 'approaching democracy' given the wide scope for debate about applying such concepts to any policy issue.[9] Does for example an annual budget or tax system provide for sufficient equality or freedom?

Nevertheless Winston Churchill anticipated the modern consensus when he said that democracy is the worst form of government except for all the others.

The Australian colonial legislatures developing new Constitutions in the 1850s deliberately rejected autocracy, including most of the limitations on democracy which remained after the 'divine right of kings' was defeated with the Glorious Revolution of 1688 and the monarch forced to work with parliament, and later evolution of the British Constitution which further increased the power of Parliament.

Democracies are the result of such events, but in the final measure, democracy is about the dignity of ordinary people.

Notes

1 (1863) 14 CB(NS) 180. The Wandsworth Board of Works demolished Mr. Cooper's house before seeking an explanation from him as to whether he had provided the Board with seven days' notice of construction of his house.
2 John Stuart Mill, Liberty (1859) 34 <https://socialsciences.mcmaster.ca/econ/ugcm/3ll3/mill/liberty.pdf>.
3 A.C.V. Melbourne, *Early Constitutional Development in Australia* (St Lucia, University of Queensland Press, 1963), 444.
4 Sir Ivor Jennings, *The British Constitution* (Cambridge University Press, 1858 ed.), 216.
5 Boyle Travers Finniss, The Constitutional History of South Australia during Twenty-One Years, from the Foundation of the Settlement in 1836 to the Inauguration of Responsible Government in 1857, W.C. Rigby, 1886, 217.
6 Joseph Rayner Stephens on Chartism (historyhome.co.uk); when he spoke at Kersal Moore, Manchester, accessed May 2024.
7 Finniss, The Constitutional History of South Australia during Twenty-One Years, from the Foundation of the Settlement in 1836 to the Inauguration of Responsible Government in 1857, 259.
8 John Keane, *The Life and Death of Democracy* (Simon & Schuster UK Ltd, 2009), 506–7.
9 Larry Berman and Bruce Allen Murphy, *Approaching Democracy*, 2nd ed. (Pearson Prentice Hall, 2008), 7.

Bibliography

Books

Berman, Larry, and Bruce Allen Murphy. *Approaching Democracy*, 2nd ed. Pearson Prentice Hall, 2008.
Finniss, Boyle Travers, The Constitutional History of South Australia during Twenty-One Years, from the Foundation of the Settlement in 1836 to the Inauguration of Responsible Government in 1857, W.C. Rigby 1886.

Jennings, Sir Ivor. *The British Constitution.* Cambridge University Press, 1858.

Keane, John. *The Life and Death of Democracy.* Simon & Schuster UK Ltd, 2009.

Melbourne, A.C.V. *Early Constitutional Development in Australia.* St Lucia, University of Queensland Press, 1963.

Mill, John Stuart. Liberty (1859).

Other

Cooper v. Wandsworth Board of Works (1863) 14 CB(NS) 180.

Stephens, Joseph Rayner, 24 September 1838, speech at Kersal Moor, Manchester, https://web.archive.org/web/20080219044548/http://www.victorianweb.org/history/chartism.html, accessed April 2023.

2   The 1850s constitutions and electoral laws

Abstract

Self-government for the Australian colonies was not mentioned in the Australian Constitutions Act 1850 but at the insistence of the colonists Britain accepted that self-government would be a result of the new constitution making. What form would the self-government take? Self-government began in South Australia in 1856 with one man, one vote, and the secret ballot, and in New South Wales (NSW) and Victoria in 1855 with something less than that, with one man, one vote, and the secret ballot later introduced in 1858 and 1857, respectively. Restrictions on democracy remained, including women did not have the right to vote, less democratic Legislative Councils with property qualifications for voting, or nominated, unequal electorates weighted towards more conservative country regions, multiple voting, and remaining British powers.

What were the 1850s constitutions?

Britain introduced the Australian Constitutions Act 1850 (UK) which enabled one-third nominated two-thirds elected Legislative Councils in its Australian colonies to in effect draft new constitutions reserved for the Royal Assent.[1] What was the outcome?

Self-government was not mentioned in the Act. At the insistence of the local Legislative Councils, in 1852 the British accepted that the constitutions could provide for 'responsible government' or self-government.[2] Each new constitution did so.

In 1844 a select committee led by William Wentworth resolved that general revenue be under the control of the Governor and Legislative Council, and:

> That an humble Address be presented to Her Majesty, beseeching Her Majesty to direct that the Government of this Colony be henceforth conducted on the same principle of responsibility, as to Legislative control, which has been conceded in the Canadas …

After the 1850 Act was proclaimed the New South Wales Legislative Council resolved that the Imperial Parliament not have the power to tax the

DOI: 10.4324/9781003490739-3

Figure 2.1 The first ministry under responsible Government. NSW 22 May, 1856 (left to right): Thomas Holt (1811–1888), treasurer; Sir William Manning (1811–1895), attorney-general; Sir Stuart Donaldson (1812–1867), premier; Sir John Darvall (1809–1883), solicitor-general; and George Robert Nichols (1809–1857), auditor-general and secretary for works.

colony, and that 'Customs and all other Departments should be subject to the direct supervision and control of the Colonial Legislature, which should have the appropriation of the Gross Revenues of the Colony', and that 'offices of trust and emolument should be conferred only on the settled inhabitants, the office of Governor alone excepted ...'

These demands were conceded 'in a general way' by Sir John Pakington, then Secretary of State for the Colonies in a dispatch dated 15 October 1852, and his successor the Duke of Newcastle on 18 January 1853.[3]

By 1856–1858 all men (aged 21 or over) had the vote, the secret ballot had been implemented and there were elected self-governing parliaments in the British colonies of South Australia (1856),[4] Victoria (1857),[5] and New South Wales (1858).[6] The vote came later in Queensland (1872), Western Australia (1893), and Tasmania (1896). Aboriginal people and Chinese and other ethnic groups were discussed and deliberately given the vote.

These were provincial democracies, not nations with foreign affairs powers.

The Premier, the Cabinet, the relationship between Governors and the Premier, the relationship between the Government and Legislative Assembly, parliamentary procedures, were largely not dealt with in the written constitution but were developed in each colony guided by unwritten British constitutional practice.

In each colony a parliament consisting of a Legislative Assembly and a Legislative Council was established with wide legislative powers with respect to local affairs, including control of crown lands. Election of members was provided for.

Restrictions on democracy remained, including women did not have the right to vote, less democratic and obstructive Legislative Councils, unequal electorates weighted towards more conservative country regions, plural voting, and remaining British powers. The Councils tried and failed to restrict British powers to disallow legislation.

The NSW Constitution Act 1855 (UK) and the Victoria Constitution Act 1855 (UK) received the Royal Assent on 16 July 1855. The South Australian Constitution Act 1856 (SA) received the Royal Assent in June 1856.

These constitutions continue in operation today:

> The resulting acts established some of the lasting characteristics of the State constitutions. Some of their provisions are still in force, consolidated and re-enacted in the present Constitution Acts.[7]

They were a marked exception to the general rule that 'very few constitutions last one hundred years without collapse.'[8]

The constitutions continued in operation without interruption for over 150 years. Mass politics developed and consolidated basic infrastructure and services, and the economy developed.

The essential elements of Australia's modern liberal democracies were established as long ago as the 1850s.

Figure 2.2 The Hon. John Basson Humffray, goldfields radical and then member of the Victorian Parliament.

Notes

1 Section 32 empowered the Legislative Councils to establish a Legislative Council and a House of Representatives and electoral provisions, subject to reservation for the Royal Assent.
2 A. C. V. Melbourne, Early Constitutional Development in Australia, University of Queensland Press 1963, 388
3 Silvester, EK, ed. *New South Wales Constitution Bill: The Speeches, in the Legislative Council of New South Wales, on the Second Reading of the Bill for Framing a New Constitution for the Colony*, 1853, iv–vii.
4 Constitution Act 1856 (SA), South Australian Constitution 1856, an Act to establish a Constitution for South Australia, and to grant a Civil List to Her Majesty 1856, clauses 6 and 16.
5 Victorian Constitution 1855, Electoral Act 1857 (Vic), clauses II and III.
6 New South Wales Constitution Act 1855 (UK), Electoral Reform Act 1858 (NSW), clause 9.
7 John Waugh, "Framing the First Victorian Constitution, 1853–5 [1997]," *Monash University Law Review* 21; 23, no. 2 (1997): 331–32.
8 Greg Craven, The Founding Fathers: Constitutional Kings or Colonial Knaves, Papers on Parliament No.21, December 1993, no page reference.

Bibliography

Constitution Act 1856 (SA), South Australian Constitution 1856, An Act to establish a Constitution for South Australia, and to grant a Civil List to Her Majesty 1856.

Craven, Greg. The Founding Fathers: Constitutional Kings or Colonial Knaves, Papers on Parliament No.21, December 1993.

McMinn, W. G. *A Constitutional History of Australia*. Melbourne: Oxford University Press, 1979.

New South Wales Constitution Act 1855 (UK), Electoral Reform Act 1858 (NSW).

Victorian Constitution 1855 (UK), Electoral Act 1857 (Vic).

Waugh, John. "Framing the First Victorian Constitution, 1853–5 [1997]" *Monash University Law Review* 23, no. 2 (1997).

3 The ideas that formed these new Australian colonial democracies

Abstract

The 1850s debates were conducted within a British framework and political spectrum. Members of the Legislative Councils were not censored either before they were elected or in speaking. They discussed democratisation by amending the British Constitution to include the Chartist demands, votes for all men (and even women), the secret ballot or John Bull declaring your vote, illiterate voters, Chinese, Aboriginal, and German voters, equal electorates or weighting towards the country interests, multiple voting, elected, nominated, or less democratic Legislative Councils to review 'hasty' legislation, shorter terms of parliament, and State aid to religion. In so doing they tried to address the specific circumstances of their colony. An old-fashioned Whiggery that sought constitutions that recognised and balanced all the interests of the colony, property as well as population, clashed with the coming liberalism.

The British Constitution and the Chartists – introduction

It was not a coincidence that the new liberal democracies that came from the colonial Australian Constitution and electoral law making in 1855–1858 and which still operate today as Australian States closely resembled the British Westminster system amended as the Chartists demanded with respect to three points of their Charter, votes for all men and the secret ballot, and annual parliaments became shorter parliaments. The first idea in the 1850s constitutional and electoral Act debates was the British Constitution and Chartist style radical amendments to it.

Britain willing to grant the privileges of British liberties to colonies

The bicameral democratically elected House of Burgesses was established in the North American colony of Virginia in 1642.[1] William Wentworth said as early as 1819:

> The colony of New South Wales is, I believe, the only one exclusively inhabited by Englishmen, in which there is not at least a shadow of a free government, as it possesses neither Council, a House of Assembly, nor even the privilege of trial by jury.[2]

DOI: 10.4324/9781003490739-4

CHAIRING THE MEMBER, OR THE TRIUMPHANT GUY.

Figure 3.1 Chairing the member, or the triumphant guy, cartoon of a candidate being chaired

The Durham Report of 1839 into the insurrection in Britain's colonies in loyalist Canada, a much lesser version of the American Revolution, recommended self-government for British colonists.[3] This was eventually conceded in for example Canada, Australia, and New Zealand.

The British constitution and the Chartists – what were they?

The British Parliament consisted of a House of Commons elected by men of property, perhaps 20 per cent of adult males,[4] the unelected House of Lords composed of the aristocracy, and the Monarch. The Chartists were working-class radicals in Britain who campaigned for over a decade in the mid-19th century to introduce the People's Charter, which would amend the British constitution to provide that

- all men should have the vote (universal manhood suffrage)
- voting should be by secret ballot
- electorates should be of equal numbers of voters
- Members of Parliament should be paid
- the property qualification for becoming a Member of Parliament should be abolished
- parliamentary elections should be held annually, not every seven years (this became shorter parliaments, such as three year or five years).[5]

The Prime Minister and Cabinet, and the Government's responsibility to the House of Commons, became British constitutional practice with the monarch's discretion to independently choose both lessening. Britain's constitution was partly written, partly unwritten.

The Charter was a list of radical proposals which had been discussed before but brought together and given national prominence in a strong national campaign. The UK radical Member of Parliament John Wilkes (1725–1797), for example, advocated votes for all men and in 1771 was able to change laws to enable the press to freely report debate in parliament.

There were other issues the Chartists discussed such as land reform, which became crucial campaigns in both Britain and its Australian colonies later in what were agricultural and pastoral economies. However, overall the view was that political reform would answer 'the cry of pent-up millions suffering under a diseased condition of society,' as Thomas Carlyle said, or address 'the political and social welfare of the working classes of this country' as a Chartist leader, Philip McGrath, said in 1845.[6]

The first two points of the Charter were implemented in the 1850s in three of Britain's Australian colonies but not in Britain until the early 20th century, while annual parliaments became shorter parliaments, of three (South Australia) or five (NSW and Victoria) years rather than seven.[7]

Colonists British subjects and attached to Britain

The Legislative Council members were British subjects, nearly all ethnically British or Irish. Some such as the colony Governors were 'Anglo-Australians' rather than permanent residents of the colonies or were simply British. Stuart Donaldson, the first self-governing Premier in NSW, Robert Lowe, JLFV ('alphabet') Foster, and William Wentworth went 'home' permanently after a political career in NSW and Victoria.[8] Life in the Australian colonies was for them in part a means of earning a fortune like the convict Abel Magwitch in Dickens' *Great Expectations*, or steps in a career, although like Wentworth they might also have a passionate attachment to their colony. The most radical of the colonies, South Australia, had a near majority of colonists born in Britain or Ireland while the 1856 constitution was drafted.[9]

Patriotic forms while making revolutionary change

One accepted means in British history of providing stable but radical change was to adhere to ancient patriotic forms. As Macauley said of the Glorious Revolution of 1688,

> As our Revolution was a vindication of ancient rights, so it was conducted with strict attention to ancient formalities. In almost every word and act may be discerned a profound reverence for the past. The Estates of the

Realm deliberated in the old halls and according to the old rules .... It finally decided the great question whether the popular element ... should be destroyed by the monarchical element, or should be suffered to develop itself freely, and to become dominant.[10]

Patriotic British forms were followed in the 1850s debates.

The constraints of the British political system

The Constitution makers operated within the constraints of the British political system. This included the Governors and Colonial Office, British Parliament, political opinion in Britain, political opinion in each colony composed as they were mainly of British subjects, and the Act governing the making of our new Constitutions, the Australian Constitutions Act 1850 (UK).

The British political system empowered the colonial Legislative Councils to develop local constitutions, provided a remarkably broad freedom of debate about those constitutions, and endorsed constitutions which gave all men the vote, including Aboriginal men and Chinese, and the secret ballot, as well as ending Government funding of churches.

The British political system would not have endorsed the Great Terror of the French Revolution (1793–1794), which closed all churches, set up a new Cult of Reason, renamed the months of the year, executed many citizens without crime proved by due legal process, and executed the King, and presumably would not have supported a republic or separation from Britain without great difficulty.

The threat of revolution

Behind the loyal formal speeches however were indications that loyalty to Britain was conditional on real self-government. The influential editor of the South Australia Register, Stephens, for example, called the 1850 Act 'humbug' because he thought it involved continuing British control:

We would sooner be alienated from the mother country altogether than bow to these conditions. Next door to municipal independence is absolute independence so why not go the whole way for after all, the prosperity of every nation is almost in exact ratio to the amount of control it possesses over its own affairs.[11]

The American Revolution and the smaller Canadian insurrections were known to the colonists, as were the revolutions in Europe of 1830 and 1848. The Chartists were closely watched to ascertain if they too would be violent. The poverty of the old country meant that the threat of revolution was a real one.

Protestant dissenters disliked or even hated the established church and its taxes, Scots and Welsh brought the grudges of the old world to the colonies, or colonists hated the British class system, or disliked the absence of self-government, or were republicans such as J.D. Lang and George Strickland Kingston. Bishop Short of Adelaide called those elected in 1851 'men who emigrated from England with embittered political and religious feelings, and who seek to assimilate this Colony in its habits and notions to the United States.'[12] Many influential opponents of democracy such as William Wentworth and John Baker supported self-government and were strong opposition to the local governor. They were not 'toadies.'

The public patriotism was complicated and even ambivalent.

Yet it was also very real on occasion. The mother of a small bugler boy allowed to enrol in the army aged 14 told Audrey Tennyson, wife of the Governor of South Australia, that 'his love for the Queen had always been really very remarkable.'[13] This was just before federation. Charles Dilke travelled the colonies and thought that an explanation for the democracy of the Australian colonies was that all aspired to be gentlemen, and did not reject the class system, but no one would agree to be placed beneath anyone else.[14]

The early settlers, groping in the dark for better institutions, found comfort in patriotism and loyalty all the while striking out in the most radical directions then known in the respectable British political spectrum. As in the Glorious Revolution in 1688, they followed ancient forms while engaging in radical action.

The 1850s debates and the British constitution

William Wentworth in NSW celebrated the new Britannia in his own prize-winning poetry while debating a new Constitution in the Legislative Council[15]:

'And Australasia float, with flag unfurled,
A New Britannia in another world!
(Enthusiastic cheering, the gallery joining in the applause)'

The more radical Henry Parkes, who had been a Chartist in England, supported the British Constitution and its liberties and in 1843 published a poem:

Thanksgiving of Workers for British Liberty ... at the red forge, or the loom, or in the field, Whate'er the demagogue's, the despot's Scheme.[16]

During debate in the Legislative Council in NSW in 1853, the Postmaster General said that the Bill was 'to frame a constitution for the land of my adoption, closely assimilated to that of Great Britain ... this is the closest approximation to the institutions of our forefathers ... the measure approaches nearer to the British constitution than any other we can devise.'[17]

Speaking in the Victorian Legislative Council, JLFV ('alphabet') Foster said in 1854 that[18]:

Sir, it is another fundamental principle of the British Constitution, that legislation should take place through the intervention of two Houses of Parliament and the Crown, and therefore I proceed now to point out how far we have been enabled to follow the British Constitution in the construction of an Upper House, to be in some respect analogous to the House of Lords.

The more radical Mr. O'Shanassy was also fundamentally influenced by the British Constitution but did so by referring to Daniel O'Connell's views, an important Irish leader[19]:

that it is desirable there should be three independent and co-existent powers to govern people of British origin with wisdom and justice is, I believe, as certain as any truth to be laid down in political science, and therefore I think there can be no doubt that it is necessary for us to establish and create three powers.

The most influential Irish leaders such as Daniel O'Connell did not then openly support Irish independence from Britain and were influential in Australia amongst Irish colonists,[20] although there were some more radical locals, including Scots and Welsh, who brought the grudges of the old country with them.

In the 1853 South Australian debates, Mr. Torrens said the British Constitution had tried and proved and afforded more true liberty than that of any other country now existing or that ever had existed. Mr. Davenport said that a nominated Upper House was most in accordance with the British Constitution, and the analogy of the British Constitution was the best they could adopt. The House of Lords had displayed more talent, tact, and knowledge in expounding the law than the House of Commons, because of an aristocracy of mind.[21]

Some even at this early time discussed separation and a federation of Australian colonies.[22] Mr. Darvall said during the debates on the NSW Constitution that an elected legislature will continue the connection with Britain and make it easier when the time to separate comes: 'the time may come when a severance of that connection must take place … an elective Legislature will be more conducive to that continuance, and when the time of separation from the parent state does come it will render the separation easier.'[23]

However Earl Grey's proposals for a federation of the Australian colonies had little support. J.D Lang established a republican 'Australia League' and published an appeal for the United States of Australia in 1852, which also had little support.[24] As Mr. Hay said to the Victorian Legislative Assembly in 1858, people were more attached to Britain than to their colonies or the other colonies:

> There was no such particular affection for the colony of Victoria, or of New South Wales, or of South Australia, as was had for their country by the inhabitants of Britain. They all felt and the same remark was applicable to the native-born population they all felt themselves to be more British than anything else. They might feel that they had a country-Australia-that they could claim as their own, but it mattered little to them with this feeling, whether they resided in Victoria or in New South Wales.[25]

Many expressly rejected the example of other European or New World countries. William Wentworth said,[26]

> He says that the people of this country have a right to the British Constitution. I admit they have a right to it. But neither more or less. They have no right to a Yankee Constitution of an elective Upper Chamber, which is now insisted on (hear, hear).

Mr. Parker said that

> The whole scope of the arguments in the house have been as between the British Constitution and other Constitutions .... I do not want to go to America, or to Belgium, or to any other country for a Constitution (cheers). I am satisfied to live under the Constitution of England; and it appears to me that all we have to do is to fall back upon the nearest resemblance to that Constitution we can devise.[27]

During debates many other forms of Government were referred to, particularly the United States of America and Canada.[28]

No support was expressed in the colonial Legislative Councils for the Russian or Austro-Hungarian, Ottoman, Chinese, or Japanese systems of absolute monarchy or autocracy as models.

Votes for all men

Introduction to votes for all men

Thomas Babington Macaulay, the great historian and Whig politician, said in 1842 in response to the People's Charter that without an educated electorate that understood the need to support property rights, giving all men the vote would result in the destruction of property and society. It would result in 'general anarchy and plunder.'[29] On the other hand, the same violence meant to many such as George Strickland Kingston in South Australia that there would be further riots and violence if votes for all men were *not* granted.[30]

The Australian colonial systematic attempt to limit voting to men of property in each colony was modelled on the limited electorate for the British House of Commons.

But the electorate of the House of Commons was complicated, traditional, and unsystematic (e.g. the Duke of Devonshire renounced his 'burgage votes' in 1832, 'pot boilers' could vote[31]). It was also thoroughly discredited in the eyes of some by the 16 largest constituencies of England (e.g. London, Liverpool, Manchester, Birmingham, Bristol, Leeds, Wolverhampton, and Sheffield) containing half the population and only returning 33 members of the House of Commons, while the other half returned 290. It was not based on population but on tradition.[32]

Votes for all men therefore required not minor but fundamental and radical Chartist or even Jacobin change to the Constitution, as Macaulay suggests. The background of radicalism, also known to colonists, included the People's Charter, the French Revolution which ended the absolute monarchy of France, the American Revolution which ended British rule in the name of liberty, and the revolutions of 1830 and 1848 which ended the rule of conservative or reactionary governments throughout Europe, including Prince Metternich in Austria.

The 1850s debates on votes for all men

The arguments put in the 1850s parliaments when introducing votes for all men included the alleged dangers of democracy in action and the need for a restraining influence, or even that it was an equivalence to the violence and horror of the French Revolution. On the other side arguments also included democracy and votes for all men as a natural right, representation based on population not property, the need to restore the ancient Anglo-Saxon liberties of the witan, and implicitly and perhaps overwhelmingly the support in each colony for full voting rights in the cities, and on the more radical goldfields. But democracy should also be restrained. In 1856 William Haines in the Victorian Legislative Assembly said he did not support 'naked democracy'[33] while arguing for property qualifications for both houses of Parliament.

In Victoria Mr. Fyfe spoke to the Victorian Legislative Assembly in 1856 and referred to the 'sovereignty of the people,' man had a right to political privileges, which was 'the law of nature which is anterior to all written law; he believed in moral right which is or ought to be the foundation of all social or political law; and by the express provision of the great charter of English liberty, everything that a man possessed was absolutely his own, and to take away anything from him without his consent, is a violation of this great original law of nature, and of the rights of man; and it was for the protection of this great natural and moral right that the elective franchise was conferred, and a representative form of government created. If a man were deprived of those rights and yet compelled to pay towards the public revenue, an injustice was perpetrated on him. Strictly speaking, a property qualification gave a man no right at all. It gave him influence, and would perhaps influence elections, as the man who spent the most money on an election would in all probably gain it.'[34]

In NSW Premier Cowper said to the Assembly that in discussing the Constitution Bill he had argued for a system of representation 'based on population, not property,' the principle of this Bill as well.[35]

The Leader of the Opposition Mr. Donaldson replied that the Bill[36]

was a revolution, not a reform. The bill proposed to give a power which he defied hon. members to produce a parallel to in the whole civilised world. There were plenty of examples of despotic governments yielding to popular influences. They could produce examples of despotic governments yielding to revolution for instance, France had given way by reason of a revolution. But what was the result that they had a more despotic government than they had when Louis XVI. was deposed.

He said that the Bill would

create a Legislative Assembly that had the absolute power of making the Constitution of the country. The Legislative Assembly would then be a convention in every sense of the word, and as dangerous and as damnable as that of 1789 as destructive of property and as destructive of liberty. That was his belief, and as long as he expressed what he believed to be the truth, he would not hesitate to say what he thought. They were about to create a convention in the country with no check whatever upon its democratic tendencies.

Mr. Campbell (Colonial Treasurer) gave a more wide-ranging and reasoned speech than Premier Cowper supporting the Bill[37]:

He said that the grand principle of representation according to population- a principle which the ancient Saxons tried hard to workout. And would anybody tell him that the ancient Saxons were revolutionary? He denied it. (Laughter.) The simple object of the bill was to give every honest man a vote; and when he came to consider the dispersion of population, he was at a loss to perceive how the representation could have been more equitably apportioned than it was in the bill. He could not possibly see that nine members were too many for a city like Sydney, containing as it did 80,000 souls, and treasure in the coffers of the bank to the extent of about £6,000,000 sterling.

This is a revival of the nationalistic Whig and Chartist narrative that reform of the Constitution was reviving the liberties of the ancient Saxons.

In South Australia George Strickland Kingston said on 21 November 1855 that 'the people will not be content with anything less' than votes for all men, and to deny it would be 'to continue excitement and agitation,' while on 3 November 1855 *The Register* warned that 'monster meetings' and 'monster petitions' would follow rejection of votes for all men.[38] On 22 September 1852 Francis Dutton gave notice he would move an amendment to An Act to establish the Legislative Council of South Australia a motion:

a   '(a) To extent the Franchise to every male inhabitant of this Colony, of twenty-one years of age, who shall not be legally disqualified, and who shall be registered for six months in the Electoral District for which he seeks to exercise his vote, previous to the day of such Election taking place.

b   That Votes for the Election of Members of Council be taken by Ballot.

c   That the qualification of Members elected to serve in the Legislative Council be abolished.'

During the 1851 election in South Australia in East Torrens, George Marsden Waterhouse said that 'the first and paramount right of every man was to have a voice in the government of the country. It was a right of human nature ....' Many similar statements were made in support of democracy on the hustings in that election campaign. It seemed difficult in fact to be elected without such support.

The concept of votes for men would not apply to convicts, because transportation of convicts to NSW ended in 1840, and Van Diemen's Land in 1853. Transportation to Western Australia continued until 1868.

Aboriginal, Chinese, German, and others not of British ethnic origin or heritage[39]

Aboriginal, Chinese, and German men, and others not of British heritage were given the vote and were not excluded, a startling thing for the world at that time. They had more entitlements than the 80 per cent of ethnically British men who were excluded from voting in Britain itself.[40] The vote was given despite for example conflicts with Chinese people on the goldfields and elsewhere, and conflicts with Aboriginal people,[41] and despite restrictions on the immigration of Chinese introduced in Victoria in 1855 and NSW in 1861. However, South Australia did not introduce such restrictions and many Chinese landed in South Australia and walked to the goldfields.[42]

Aboriginal voting was discussed in the South Australian Legislative Council in 1855 during debates on the constitution[43] and Chinese voting was called for during South Australian election rallies in 1855.[44] In 1856 Premier Haines in the Victorian Legislative Assembly said he supported voting by 'the natives of every country under heaven,' especially by those of 'the United States, and those countries of Europe who enjoyed the same constitution, professed the same religion, and in many instances spoke the same languages as themselves,' particularly the 10,000 natives of Germany on the goldfields, as well as Chinese.[45] Miners were given specific voting rights in NSW and Victoria, and the involvement of nationals from many countries in the goldfields was widely discussed, even notorious.

Debating the Parliament Bill in the South Australian Legislative Council in 1855, Mr. Reynolds said that he was aware of an Aboriginal person voting in a previous election in West Torrens (and voting against him), which he expressed no difficulty with and said demonstrated that the new bill conferred no powers on Aboriginal people that they did not already have.[46] 'Several' Aboriginal men were placed on the electoral role in NSW in the 1850s,[47] and up to 100 men and women at Point McLeay in South Australia in the 1890s, of whom 70 voted in 1896.[48]

This was an enlightened contrast to the Commonwealth Franchise Act 1902 (Cth). This bill was amended to exclude 'aboriginal natives of Australia, Asia, Africa or the Islands of the Pacific' from being placed on the electoral roll unless they were eligible to vote under state legislation in accordance with Section 41 of the Australian Constitution. The bill had originally included them. It would be another 60 years before all Aboriginal and Torres Strait Islander people were able to enrol and vote at federal elections, following the 1962 amendment of the Commonwealth Electoral Act 1918 (Cth) (which replaced the Franchise Act 1902).[49]

Queensland restricted Aboriginal voting rights in 1885. This was not disallowed by the Colonial Office, although the Colonial Office in 1876 disallowed the harsh Queensland Goldfields (Amendment) Bill which restricted Chinese from mining. The Colonial Office did not disallow 1880s legislation in four colonies which virtually excluded Chinese mining. British willingness to disallow had waned with consolidation of local democracy, despite 'traditions of a multi-racial empire,' including India.[50]

Such is the remarkable obscurity of the 1850s electoral debates that occasionally it is assumed in even the best researched books and articles that the Australian legislators of the 1850s did not realise that they were giving Aboriginal men, Chinese, Germans, and others voting rights.[51]

Women could vote in South Australian local government elections from 1861, and some women voted in 1864 Victorian parliamentary elections because municipal voting rolls were used. In Britain legislation in 1869 gave women the right to vote in municipal elections, limited in 1872 to unmarried ratepayers. There was practical experience with women voting, 'anomalies' which Woollacott said helped Catherine Spence and others later campaigning for votes for women and which countered 'gendered' assumptions.[52]

Votes for women were occasionally discussed during the 1850s debates. For example, Mr. Michie in the Victorian Legislative Assembly said in 1856 that he supported votes for women and said he knew many who were 'much better fitted for exercise of the franchise than members of the male sex.'[53]

Aboriginal people before colonisation had their own very different laws and methods of government based on transmission of ancestral law, kinship networks and power differences based largely on age and gender, and ceremonies and ritual which were gradually displaced.[54] Only some, perhaps very few, Aboriginal men voted under the colonial Acts. There was no compulsion for anyone to vote, and Aboriginal law and custom mostly remained a key influence for them although there were early Aboriginal petitions for example for land but possibly not votes.[55]

Few people voted in any event; only about one quarter of the electoral role voted for the first responsible Government in 1856 in South Australia, for example. South Australia also promoted orderly and dignified debate by prohibiting candidates from attending political meetings in the electorates they were contesting. Instead candidates wrote letters to the newspapers outlining their platforms and record of service.[56]

Nor was there ever a formal institution of slavery in the Australian colonies, although there were British and Irish convicts in colonies other than South Australia, and a form of bonded labour for South Sea islanders in Queensland.[57]

Secret ballot

The arguments put included the unanimous opinion of the colony in favour of the secret ballot, to protect voters against coercion given the potential consequences if a vote was known, and people with power or influence knew this and objected and even acted to the voter's detriment, and the John Bull argument that it was cowardly and un-English to be secret in voting, when votes had always been and should be publicly stated and stoutly defended as Englishmen should.

In the South Australian Legislative Council, the Advocate-General, R.D. Hanson, then moved an amendment on 20 February 1856 to provide for the secret ballot, to protect voters against 'coercion,' and as the opinion of the people was so 'decidedly pronounced' on the issue. The Speaker, Fisher, said that he had an 'insuperable objection' to the secret ballot and that this new experiment would be tested and be found to be a failure, and he wanted his name on the record as opposing it when it was found to be a failure.[58] The secret ballot passed.

In the NSW Legislative Assembly, Mr. Campbell[59] said in 1858 that he was also in favour of vote by ballot, as proposed in the bill, because he believed it was the 'safest protection they could afford the poor against the intimidation of the rich.'

In the Legislative Council of NSW, Deas Thomson said the secret ballot was a necessary safeguard against working-class intimidation of those of their number who voted for conservative candidates: 'No labouring man would dare to vote against his class. If he did he would become a pariah and an outcast.'[60]

Figure 3.2 Sir James Hurtle Fisher, ca. 1870

Sir James Stephen told the NSW Legislative Council in 1858[61] that some said that the secret ballot was 'un-English and cowardly' because they sought to avoid the 'rotten eggs and cabbages' thrown during voting and speeches, during the public spectacle and occasional riot of public voting under the old system.

In South Australia the secret ballot was called 'unmanly' and 'un-English.' Thomas Reynolds argued that the ballot 'lay at the foundation of their liberties.'[62]

The upper house of parliament

The Chartists had no proposal to reform the House of Lords. In Britain this difficult question would be resolved in the 20th century. In 1911 its powers were limited to delaying not blocking new legislation.

A nominated upper house had been 'the usual basis for legislation for second chambers in British colonies for about two centuries,' although an elective one had been recently proposed for the Cape Colony, and William

Gladstone and other leading statement had 'favourably discussed' elective upper houses.[63]

The Secretary of State, Sir John Pakington, sent a memorandum to Governor Fitzroy of NSW on 15 December 1852 in which he advised that 'the Council should establish the new legislature on the basis of an elective Assembly and a Legislative Council to be nominated by the Crown.' He was succeeded in December 1852 by Lord Newcastle who sent a further memorandum on 18 January 1853 indicating more flexibility and who privately supported an elective upper house.[64] Copies were sent to the Lieutenant-Governors of Victoria and South Australia.

In the Australian colonies proposals included unicameralism (one house of parliament only), creation of a colonial aristocracy supported by William Wentworth in NSW and John Morphett in South Australia, a nominated upper house supported by William Wentworth and introduced into the NSW Constitution, and an upper house with property qualifications for voting and membership, as was introduced into the Victorian and South Australian Constitutions, or an upper house elected with no property qualifications as proposed by Francis Dutton in South Australia.

Wentworth was roundly mocked for his 'bunyip aristocracy' proposal, Daniel Deniehy suggesting that another purported aristocrat, James Macarthur, have a rum barrel as his heraldic coat of arms. Early NSW had used rum as currency, and after the Governor tried to control the rum trade, James' father John Macarthur led the 'rum rebellion' which deposed the Governor. John Stephens, editor of the South Australian Register, said of John Morphett, who also supported a colonial aristocracy, that

> He had reached such a stage of self-complacency and arrogance that he imagined there was something of divinity in his own creation. Surely somewhere along the line he was of noble birth.[65]

Daniel Deniehy, the author of great mirth, directed at the 'bunyip aristocrats' as he called them, was one himself. He regarded himself as a 'natural aristocrat' and 'dressed almost as a dandy,' from his 'faultlessly fitting frock coat to the tortoise shell paper knife.'[66]

William Wentworth then supported a nominated upper house, in the knowledge that this was weaker than one elected with a property qualification because it could be 'swamped' by nominations by the Governor. William Wentworth said the decision of the Lords in 1832 to pass the Electoral Reform Bill under threat of being 'swamped' was 'one of the purest efforts of the patriotism of its members' and a model for all second chambers.[67]

In Victoria and South Australia, conservatives supported an upper house elected with a property qualification for membership, and for voting. The Victorian Collector of Customs said the Upper House with property qualifications was 'a conservative element, a check upon rash and hasty legislation'[68] Mr. Foster said in justification of a requirement of property holding:

> We also having observed that wealth generally gave a man very steady ideas, thought it very desirable that in the Legislative Council we should have none but men who did possess that stake in the country; that in fact, all adventurers should be practically excluded from it. I do not think that those gentlemen whom, without any disrespect, I have termed adventurers, ought to be in the Upper House: they will have ample scope for the display of their talent and ambition in the Lower House.[69]

Wentworth the romantic British Constitutionalist was very different to 'Alphabet' Foster, the deadly realist, a political killer. Foster knew the Legislative Council he was developing could 'block any measure it disliked'[70] because of a high property qualification for voting and sitting. This it proceeded to do for the rest of the century, causing serious political crises which were only ever partly resolved.

Mr. O'Shanassy said that Legislative Council in Committee discussed a system of double election, with municipal corporations electing the Legislative Council or Senate, that the Legislative Assembly should elect the Upper, and that the Governor should be able to veto the election of Senators. Instead he had moved that the two Houses be independent of each other.[71]

In the South Australian debates in 1853 Mr. Dutton said,[72]

> How could the Upper House act harmoniously with the Lower Chamber unless the people had a voice in its formation? He was quite satisfied as to the fitness of the people, and was prepared to place the trust in their hands.

Mr. Gwynne said his fear was the fear of the tyranny of the democratic majority. Many who thought with him objected to the measure on account of its democratic tendencies. He would be willing to support the measure – to take all risks – if a nominated Upper House were conceded. If they refused a nominee Upper House, the Constitution would be nothing more nor less than a pure democracy, and they would soon sink into a republic. He wanted a similar institution to the House of Lords.

Mr. Waterhouse said a second chamber would be a check upon hasty legislation and a link between the Crown and the people. There was no analogy between a nominated Upper House and the House of Lords, nor could we compare this colony and England. People appeared to labour under the apprehension of some indefinable evil connected with an elective Upper House, but such was not a necessary feature of a republic.

Mr. Peacock said he would rather lay his head on the block than entail on his children such a farcical imitation of the House of Lords. Nineteen out of twenty colonists would be strenuously opposed to a nominee Upper House.

Mr. Richard Davies Hanson, Advocate-General, said that the House of Lords did not set themselves permanently against the people. Catholic Emancipation, the Reform Bill, and the Repeal of the Corn Laws were carried against the richest and most potent aristocracy in the world. He wanted independent men in the Upper House who did not look with one eye on merits and another on the desires of their constituents. The opinions of the people were not always correct.

In Victoria and South Australia, responsible government under the new constitutions of 1855–1856 included an elected Legislative Council with a property qualification to be eligible to vote. In NSW and Queensland, the Council was nominated by the governor. Both were a deliberate means of providing a check or limit on the more democratic Legislative Assemblies.

The Legislative Councils were a colonial equivalent of the House of Lords. However, in Victoria and to a lesser extent South Australia, the upper houses were arguably more assertive than in Britain. In Britain most leaders of the Whigs and Tories worked to avoid collisions between the Lords and the more popular house, the elected House of Commons. This was 'the conventional Whig doctrine that the conservative branch of the legislature could not indefinitely resist strong and repeated demands for change without damaging the structure of the body politic and exposing itself to the danger of being swept away by an enraged populace.'[73]

The rejection by the House of Lords of the Reform Bill 1830 led to government threats to 'swamp' the Lords with new members supportive of the government and a violent public campaign against the leader of the Tories, the Duke of Wellington, and against the Tories generally. The House of Lords gave way and passed the Reform Act 1832 (UK) which gave one in five men the vote.

In New South Wales, the Legislative Council drafted a constitution for responsible government which did not include William Wentworth's proposal for an upper house composed of a colonial hereditary peerage, instead providing for a nominated upper house, his later proposal.

Equal electorates

The electorates in all the colonies were weighted in favour of country areas, which were more conservative, and against the more radical cities. Equality of electorates was not the objective of Wentworth and others. Wentworth believed that 'representation should be based on … not the mere population … but should be so proportioned that no one interest shall have a preponderating influence over any other,'[74] an 18th-century traditional Whig view which echoed Edmund Burke and William Blackstone, who spoke of the several parts of the constitution being a 'check' on each other, prevented from exceeding their proper limits, and forcing 'perpetual' compromise.

The same language of parliament representing and balancing the different 'interests' of the colony, property as well as population or simple citizenship, was used to retain unequal electorate districts and plural voting in the Victorian 1857 Electoral Act debates. Mr. Stawell said 'He took it their object ought to be fair representation of every interest and he contended if property was not represented, one class in the community would not be represented, and then class legislation would follow,' a position supported by Premier Haines while giving all men the vote. Mr. Blair said that 'If he understood the suffrage at all, it ought to based on simple citizenship and that alone.'[75]

Of the 36 elected members in NSW in the 1851 election, 4 came from the more radical Sydney and hamlets, while 17 from counties and 8 from pastoral districts: 'the exclusive landed interest had an overwhelming majority.' The distribution of seats was similar in Victoria and South Australia.

As Premier Charles Cowper of NSW said in 1858, the existing electoral system was heavily weighted in favour of country electorates and against Sydney when reviewing in detail the distribution of voters for each seat, highlighting the large differences. He supported a reallocation of seats by population, including a large increase in the seats in Sydney.[76]

Fred Daly, a prominent Whitlam Government Minister, called it 'one sheep one vote'[77] in the 1970s when an electoral weighting towards the country areas was still in existence. It is a debate which continues today over for example the electorates in the upper houses. In November 2023 the Western Australian Parliament introduced one person, one vote to the Legislative Council and removed an imbalance which saw Perth electing only half of upper house members of Parliament although it was 75 per cent of the electors in the State.[78] In the Australian Senate the smallest State (Tasmania) with only just over half a million in population has the same number of Senators as the largest (NSW) with over 8 million. The Senate is a 'state's' house.

Illiterate voters

One problem was illiterate voters, who were argued by some to be less able to follow arguments or make decisions which were beneficial to the colony, in contrast to men of property who had a stake in the colony and were aware of the dangers of attacks on property. In South Australia Mr. Baker moved in 1855 that no man could be enrolled who could not read or write. This attracted strong opposition. Mr. Bagot said that no man should be deprived of the vote 'whose ignorance was the consequence of poverty or bad government.' Mr. Peacock said that 'there was no fear of ignorant men coming in such swarms as to swamp the colony' and that such a man 'still might be man of property and sound judgement.' Mr. Baker faced strong opposition and withdrew the amendment.[79]

In Victoria in 1857 Mr. Fellows said that the registration system involved 'educational tests' which he opposed, given that at least once dignitary in the Church in Melbourne had 'handwriting ordinary men would have very great difficulty in deciphering.'[80] Mr. Foster supported a requirement of reading and writing skills to exercise the franchise.[81]

All men would have the vote in all the colonies regardless of literacy. There was a 58 per cent literacy rate in 1858 if these early statistics are accurate (compared to 80 per cent in 1901).[82]

Property rights

The drafters understood that a new Constitution had to protect property while also allowing for a form of self-determination, and self-government. In many respects the debate was between those who supported the limited democracy of the British Constitution, which limited voting to men of property, and those who supported British radicalism and the Chartist amendments to the British Constitution, which meant all men could vote.

Non-British models. Philosophers

The debates were not confined to the Constitutions of other countries. In Victoria Premier Haines referred to John Stuart Mill while O'Shanassy implicitly to John Locke that working men were men of property because they owned their own labour.[83] William Wentworth referred to de Tocqueville on the problems in America caused by too much democracy.[84] References were made to Lang's proposed republic, Canada, the French Revolution, the Cape and the Dutch, Pitt and hereditary titles, Alexander Hamilton and Thomas Jefferson, slavery, Blackstone, Belgium, and the US Congress.[85]

British political party titles and platforms

British political terms such as conservative, liberal, radical, and Chartist were not used on all occasions to describe positions and platforms taken by colony leaders during constitutional debates.

Sometimes their use seemed paradoxical such as Stuart Donaldson's description of himself as a 'liberal-conservative.'[86] He referred to two distinct bodies of political thinking in the colonies, and his ability to draw from both. Donaldson was the first Premier of NSW under self-government in 1856.

JLFV ('alphabet') Foster denied that such labels were useful in the colonies given that they referred in Britain to certain issues such as a standing army, national debt, House of Lords, and established church, none of which were present in the colonies.[87] He supported self-government but opposed democratisation. On other occasions some did use such labels. The Chartists' platform was clearly relevant to local democratisation debates, as relevant as the British Constitution.

The Charter was in effect amended in South Australia to deal with their direct problems, namely nominees to the Legislative Council and what Protestant dissenters saw as the priority of ending State aid to religion. Chaotic discussions occurred between opponents of State aid to religion and advocates of giving all men the vote and secret ballot, resulting in candidates for the 1851 election being asked:

1   'Are you in favour of, and would you vote for, the adoption of the ballot at the elections?
2   Are you in favour of State grants for the support of religion, or would you strenuously oppose such a measure?
3   In the event of your being returned as our representative, how far would you extend the suffrage?
4   Would you use your utmost endeavours to obtain the constitution of an Assembly strictly representation, as opposed to nomination?
5   As to the duration of Legislative Councils, would you limit them to three years, or what are your views on this head?'[88]

British parliamentary and constitutional practice

Much of the substance of the new self-governing democracies, the functions of the Premier, the Cabinet, the relationship between Governors and the Premier, and between the Premier and parliament, parliamentary procedures, were not dealt with in the written constitution but were developed in each colony guided by unwritten British constitutional practice.

In Victoria British parliamentary rules were adopted in the first self-governing parliament until standing orders were developed, and Ministers resigned and recontested their seats on taking office.[89] The practice of Ministers recontesting seats was adopted in colonies other than South Australia and removed in Queensland in 1884, NSW in 1906, and Victoria in 1914.[90]

Some procedures adopted reflected struggles for the freedom and autonomy of the House of Commons such as dragging the speaker to the chair after his election, to force him to take office despite threats from the King. Other practices included the mace, black rod rapping loudly on the door, the formal office of Premier and Leader of the Opposition. The constitutional debates of the 1850s broadly followed the procedure of a formal majority or Government view followed by dissenting views.

The wife of the Governor Sir William Denison at the opening of NSW Parliament in May 1856 noted with amusement that the colony even had a State carriage drawn by four horses and driven by a coachman in borrowed livery, as in Britain itself. British forms were important to the colonists who did not see them as ludicrous but a reassuring link to ancient traditions of liberty and parliament.[91]

Religious freedom and separation of Church and State

The British and European wars of religion lingered into the 19th century. Catholics and Protestant dissenters were excluded from voting and sitting in local government and parliament in patriotically Protestant Britain with an established church until 1828. Britain required payment of church rates and taxes. Some British settlers, particularly Protestant dissenters such as William Giles, and the League for the Maintenance of Religious Freedom in South Australia brought this debate to South Australia and the other colonies. The League was successful in including an end to State aid in a list of otherwise Chartist questions to be asked of candidates in the 1851 election, although the Chartists in Britain did not have a position on State aid to religion:

> Are you in favour of State grants for the support of religion, or would you strenuously oppose such a measure?

This was one of the most contentious issues if not the most contentious in that election, along with the secret ballot. Candidates were closely questioned on this issue.[92]

After the election the Legislative Council voted to end State aid to religion in 1851, the first colony in the empire to do so. First, on 29 August 1851, a Bill to provide funds for church building and maintenance of Christian ministers was defeated. Mr. Finniss said that Christianity was part and parcel of the law of the land. Why should the State be excluded by law from supporting it? George Hall (who claimed he was 'practically' a voluntarist to get elected) supported the first reading, a community so blessed and favoured by Providence should not refuse to devote a portion of its wealth to the service of God. It was the first step to throwing off allegiance to the King of Kings.

Mr. Baker said that country districts should be supported by State aid. He beseeched members not to throw the Bill out without due discussion, and great injury would be done to the colony if this was noised abroad. Mr. Dutton said that it would be advisable to reject it without long discussion.

Then on 19 December 1851, Kingston moved in the Legislative Council that Ecclesiastical grants are illegal. This was passed.[93]

This ended State aid for religion in South Australia.[94] The debate in Britain was more difficult. It had for example the issue of a Protestant established church in Catholic Ireland to deal with. South Australia would never have an established church.[95]

State aid to religion continued in New South Wales until 1862,[96] in Victoria until 1870, and in Western Australia until 1895.[97]

Control of Crown lands and local affairs

Self-government meant government of most things apart from foreign affairs. Local governors were guided by Royal Instructions which forbade them to give assent to certain matters such as restrictions on freedom of religion, and the granting of divorce.

Parliamentarians were in favour of the new self-governing parliaments having control of Crown lands, including their revenue. Without such control, the new governments would have had more difficulty in developing agricultural and pastoral affairs and other aspects of their economies.

For example, this was the first recommendation of William Wentworth's Select Committee on the NSW Constitution in 1853.[98]

During the 1851 election in South Australia in East Torrens, George Marsden Waterhouse supported the secret ballot and universal suffrage, opposed State aid, but denied he was the representative of the League. He said that 'the first and paramount right of every man was to have a voice in the government of the country. It was a right of human nature …. The most important interest was the agricultural interest, which he would promote by opening up new roads in the colony and new markets, not by imposing duties on corn exported to foreign states.'[99]

Other

The terms of parliament would be shorter than the seven years maximum in Britain, but not the Chartist annual parliaments or recall of members on petition. South Australia adopted three year parliaments, while the other parliaments five year terms.[100]

Plural voting, the ability to vote in multiple electorates where the voter had a property was justified on the basis that laws had to recognise property as well as population. As Mr. Fellows told Victorian parliament in 1858 'The only way to keep the balance of representation was to allow property to be represented as well as individuals.' Mr. Owens disagreed and said multiple voting would 'practically demolish the extension of the franchise to all.'[101] Plural or multiple voting was an entitlement in in Victoria and NSW but not in South Australia.

Payment of members was introduced later. During the 1851 election William Wentworth said NSW members would 'spurn any such payments' as in 'poor' Canada, and James Macarthur that such Canadian payments would lead to 'shameful conduct' and 'a tyranny such as has never oppressed the country in its worst days.'[102]

The debates were conducted under the authority of a British Act of Parliament, and sovereignty derived from settlement in 1788. Some form of separation from Britain was occasionally mentioned as a future possible question. There was no general discussion of sovereignty.

Table 3.1 Payment of members

Vic	1877–1883
NSW	1889
Qld	1889
SA	1890
Tas	1891
WA	1900
Britain	1911

Source: McMinn, *Constitutional History*, Melbourne, Oxford University Press, 1979, p. 64

Notes

1 18 February 1819, Sir James Macintosh, House of Commons, Debates, 18 February 1819, Hansard Third Series, vol. 39, 496–97.

2 William Wentworth, *A Statistical, Historical and Political Description of the Colony of New South Wales* (London, 1819), quoted in *Edward Sweetman, Australian Constitutional Development* (Macmillan & Co Limited in association with Melbourne University Press, 1925), 21.

3 http://eco.canadiana.ca/view/oocihm.32374/2?r=0&s=1, accessed May 2024.

4 John A. Phillips and Charles Wetherell, "The Great Reform Act of 1832 and the Political Modernisation of England," *The American Historical Review* 100, no. 2 (Apr.1993): 414.

5 Asa Briggs, ed., *Chartist Studies* (The Macmillan Press Ltd, 1959), 23–24.

6 Briggs, ed., *Chartist Studies*, 1959, 25, 309.

7 NSW Constitution 1855 clause XXI, Victorian Constitution 1855 clause XIX, South Australian Constitution clause 3.

8 Wentworth died in Britain and was buried in Australia.

9 Hamilton, *Colony*, 2010, 217.

10 Thomas Babbington Macaulay, *The Revolution, George Otto Trevalyan, MP, Selections from the Writings of Lord Macauley* (London: Longmans, Green and Co, 1883), 266–68.

11 Russell Smith, *1850, A Very Good Year in the Colony of South Australia* (Sydney: Shakespeare Head Press, 1973), 62.

12 Hamilton, *Colony*, 2010, 225.

13 Audrey Tennyson's Vice-Regal Days, Alexandra Hasluck, ed., *National Library of Australia* (Canberra, 1978), 85.

14 Hamilton, *Colony*, 2010, 216, Charles Dilke, *Greater Britain*, 1869.

15 Silvester, *NSW Legislative Council Debates, 1853*, ed. Edward Kennedy Silvester, 226.

16 Henry Parkes, *Thanksgiving of Workers for British Liberty*, 1843.

17 Silvester, *NSW Legislative Council Debates, 1853*, ed. Edward Kennedy Silvester, 203–4.

18 George H.F. Webb, *Debate in the Legislative Council of the Colony of Victoria on the Second Reading of the New Constitution Bill* (Melbourne: Caleb Turner, 1854), 9.

19 Webb, *Victorian Legislative Council Debates*, 1854, 20.

20 Webb, *Victorian Legislative Council Debates*, 1854, 20–21.

21 John Blackett, *History of South Australia* (Adelaide: Hussey & Gillingham, 1911), 256–74. This debate is taken from Blackett, who often summarises rather than quotes the debate. I have paraphrased some of the longer passages to shorten them while retaining their meaning and omitted speakers who simply supported one side or the other.

22 John La Nauze, *The Making of the Australian Constitution* (Melbourne University Press, 1972), 2.

23 Silvester, NSW *Legislative Council Debates*, 1853, ed. Edward Kennedy Silvester, 217.

24 WG McMinn, *A Constitutional History of Australia* (OUP, Melbourne, 1979), 94.

25 Sydney Morning Herald, 13 May 1858, 2.

26 Silvester, *NSW Legislative Council Debates, 1853*, ed. Edward Kennedy Silvester, 214.

27 Silvester, *NSW Legislative Council Debates, 1853*, ed. Edward Kennedy Silvester, 203–5.

28 Webb, *Victorian Legislative Council Debates*, 1854, 22–25.

29 Hansard, Vol. 63, 3 May 1842; Opposition to Universal Suffrage (historyhome. co.uk). Opposition to universal suffrage (historyhome.co.uk); accessed May 2024.

30 S Scalmer, "Containing Contention: A Reinterpretation of Democratic Change and Electoral Reform in the Australian Colonies," *Australian Historical Studies* 42, no. 3 (2011): 338, 347.

31 Sarah Richardson, *"Independence and Deference: A Study of the West Riding Electorate, 1832-1841,"* PhD thesis, 1995, 7, 187: Pot boilers were 'These were inhabitant householders who benefited from the 1783 change in the franchise. The inhabitant householders were remnants of the pre 1832 electorate and thus expected payment.' https://etheses.whiterose.ac.uk/541/1/uk_bl_ethos_249203.pdf, accessed May 2024. The University of Leeds School of History September, 1995.

32 Russell Smith, *1850, A Very Good Year in the Colony of South Australia* (Sydney: Shakespeare Head Press, 1973), 107.

33 Hansard 16 December 1856, 170.

34 Hansard 10 December 1856, 105.

35 Sydney Morning Herald, 7 May 1858, 2.

36 Sydney Morning Herald, 7 May 1858, 2–3.

37 Sydney Morning Herald, 7 May 1858, 3–4.

38 S Scalmer, "Containing Contention: A Reinterpretation of Democratic Change and Electoral Reform in the Australian colonies," *Australian Historical Studies* 42, no. 3 (2011): 338, 347.

39 Britain has always had a degree of mixed ethnic origin. For example, the Roman Empire brought people from all over the empire to Britain.

40 John A. Phillips and Charles Wetherell, "The Great Reform Act of 1832 and the Political Modernisation of England," *The American Historical Review* 100, no. 2 (Apr.1993): 414.

41 CN Connolly, *"Politics, Ideology and the New South Wales Legislative Council, 1856–72,"* PhD thesis, Australian National University, 1974, 30. https://openresearch-repository.anu.edu.au/bitstream/1885/124864/2/b10150663_Connolly_ Christopher_Newland.pdf, 162–83.

42 Chinese Immigration Act 1855 (Vic).

43 South Australian Register, 11 November 1855, 2.

44 South Australian Register, 22 September 1855.

45 Hansard, 16 December 1856, 165–66.

46 South Australian Register (Adelaide, SA: 1839–1900), 22 November 1855, 2.

47 R Therry, *Reminiscences of Thirty Years' Residence in New South Wales and Victoria,* facsimile ed. (Sydney University Press, 1974), 459,, . It should be noted that Therry uses language to describe Aboriginal people which would not be acceptable today, as did others of the time. I have not yet found such unacceptable language in the Legislative Council debates on the constitutions.

48 Australian Electoral Commission, History of the Indigenous Vote, Electoral Milestones for Indigenous Australians – Australian Electoral Commission (aec.gov.au), accessed November 2023.

49 A Hough, The 120th Anniversary of Women's Suffrage in Australia, Womens Suffrage – Parliament of Australia (aph.gov.au), accessed 6 March 2023.

50 WG McMinn, *A Constitutional History of Australia* (Melbourne: OUP, 1979), 89–90.

51 A Curthoys and J Mitchell, *Taking Liberty* (Cambridge University Press, 2020), 223: 'It is doubtful that anyone in the colonies recognised this [that Aboriginal men were included] at the time.'

52 Angela Woollacott, *Settler Society in the Australian Colonies* (Oxford University Press, 2015), 150–51.

53 Hansard, 18 December 1856, 171.

54 A Curthoys and J Mitchell, "The Advent of Self-Government," in *The Cambridge History of Australia*, ed. A Bashford and S Macintyre, vol. 1 (Cambridge University Press, 2013), 149.
55 One study found no Aboriginal petitions for voting rights until 1894. There were petitions for land and other grievances well before that: Chiara Gamboz, "*Petitions from Indigenous Australians: Emergence and Negotiations of Indigenous Authorship and Writings*," Unpublished PhD thesis, 2012, 42, downloaded from http://hdl.handle.net/1959.4/52311 in https:// unsworks.unsw.edu.au on 2023-12-17.
56 Parliament.sa.gov.au, The First Parliament. South Australia Achieves Self Government in 1857, accessed December 2024.
57 K Saunders, *Workers in Bondage: The Origins and Bases of Unfree Labour in Queensland, 1824–1916* (St. Lucia: University of Queensland Press, 1982).
58 The Register, 21 February 1856; Combe Responsible Government in Australia.
59 Sydney Morning Herald, 7 May 1858, 3–4.
60 Sydney Morning Herald, 9 September, 1858.
61 https://nla.gov.au:443/tarkine/nla.obj-645021989, accessed March 2023.
62 sahistoryhub.history.sa.gov.au, Responsible Government, accessed December 2023.
63 Edward Sweetman, *Australian Constitutional Development* (Macmillan & Co Limited in association with Melbourne University Press, 1925), 277.
64 A.C.V. Melbourne, *Early Constitutional Development in Australia* (University of Queensland Press, 1963), 399–400.
65 Russell Smith, *1850, A Very Good Year in the Colony of South Australia* (Sydney: Shakespeare Head Press, 1973), 37.
66 Melleuish, G, Daniel Deniehy, "Bede Dalley and the Ideal of the Natural Aristocrat in Colonial New South Wales," *Australian Journal of Politics & History* 33, no. 1 (April 2008):45–59.
67 Connolly, C.N., "Politics, Ideology and the New South Wales Legislative Council, 1856–72," 30. https://openresearch-repository.anu.edu.au/bitstream/1885/124864/2/b10150663_Connolly_Christopher_Newland.pdf
68 Webb, *Victorian Legislative Council Debates*, 1854, 124.
69 *Webb, Victorian Legislative Council Debates*, 1854, 14.
70 Frank Bongiorno, *Dreamers and Schemers* (Latrobe University Press, 2022), 44–45.
71 Webb, *Victorian Legislative Council Debates*, 1854, 22–25.
72 John Blackett, *History of South Australia* (Adelaide: Hussey & Gillingham, 1911), 256–74. This debate is taken from Blackett, who often summarises rather than quotes the debate. I have paraphrased some of the longer passages to shorten them while retaining their meaning and omitted speakers who simply supported one side or the other.
73 CN Connolly, "*Politics, Ideology and the New South Wales Legislative Council, 1856–72*," PhD thesis, Australian National University, 1974, 30. https://openresearch-repository.anu.edu.au/bitstream/1885/124864/2/b10150663_Connolly_Christopher_Newland.pdf
74 A.C.V. *Melbourne, Early Constitutional Development in Australia* (University of Queensland Press, 1963), 404.
75 Hansard, 16 December 1856, 167–73.
76 Sydney Morning Herald, 7 May 1858, 2.
77 Ms.Follett, Leader of the Opposition, 22 August 1995, Legislative Assembly for the Australian Capital Territory, Hansard, 1179, Hansard – ACT Legislative Assembly, accessed January 2023.
78 The Electoral Legislation Amendment (Electoral Equality) Act 2021.
79 South Australian Register 19 December 1855, 4–10.
80 Hansard 10 December 1856, 100.

81 Webb, *Victorian Legislative Council Debates*, 1854, 7.
82 Commonwealth Bureau of Census and Statistics 1908, Official Year Book of the Commonwealth of Australia No.1, McCarron, Bird & Co.
83 Hansard 18 December 1856, 167.
84 Silvester, *NSW Legislative Council Debates*, 1853, 226.
85 Silvester, *NSW Legislative Council Debates*, 1853, 34, 80, 22, 36, 41–44, 42, 53, 55, 62, 71, 93.
86 Loveday P and A.W. Martin, *Parliament Factions and Parties, The First Thirty Years of Responsible Government in New South Wales* (Melbourne University Press, 1966), 23.
87 GHF Webb, *Debate in the Legislative Council of the Colony of Victoria on the Second Reading of the New Constitution Bill* (Melbourne: Caleb Turner, 1854), 4.
88 Hamilton, *Colony*, 2010, 218–219.
89 Geoffrey Serle, *The Golden Age* (Melbourne University Press, 1977), 258, 262.
90 WG McMinn, *A Constitutional History of Australia* (Melbourne: OUP, 1979), 65.
91 McMinn, *A Constitutional History of Australia*, 1979, 58.
92 Hamilton, *Colony*, 2010, 218–19.
93 These dates, motions and resolutions are taken from 'Votes and Proceedings of the Legislative Council,' South Australia.
94 J Blackett, *History of South Australia* (Adelaide: Hussey and Gillingham, 1911), 244–46.
95 Hamilton, *Colony*, 2010, 225.
96 Wylde v Attorney General of NSW (1948) 78 CLR 224 at 257, Chief Justice Latham of the High Court of Australia.
97 D Pike, *A Paradise of Dissent: South Australia 1829–1857* (Melbourne University Press, 1967); Hamilton, *Colony*, 2010, 225.
98 Silvester New South Wales Constitution Bill: The speeches, in the Legislative Council of New South Wales, on the second reading of the bill for framing a new constitution for the colony, 1853, iii.
99 The Southern Australian, 4 July 1851; See Hamilton, *Colony*, 2010, 225.
100 Victorian Constitution 1855, clause XIX; South Australian Constitution 1856, clause 3.WG McMinn, A constitutional history of Australia, OUP, Melbourne, 1979, 64.
101 Hansard, 18 December 1856, 167–73.
102 P. Cochrane, *Colonial Ambition* (Carlton: Melbourne University Press, 2006), 439.

Bibliography

Books and PhD Thesis

Blackett, John. *History of South Australia*. Adelaide: Hussey & Gillingham, 1911.
Bongiorno, Frank. *Dreamers and Schemers*. Collingwood VIC, Australia: La Trobe University Press in conjunction with Black Inc, 2022.
Cochrane, Peter. *Colonial Ambition*. Carlton: Melbourne University Press, 2006.
Commonwealth Bureau of Census and Statistics, Melbourne, Official Year Book of the Commonwealth of Australia, Containing Authoritative Statistics for the Period 1901–1907, and corrected Statistics for the Period 1788 to 1900. No.1 – 1908. Published: Under the Authority of the Minister of Home Affairs, by G. H. Knibbs, Fellow of the Royal Statistical Society, etc., Commonwealth Statistician. By Authority. McCarron, Bird and Co., Printers, Collins Street, Melbourne.

Connolly, Christopher Newland. *"Politics, Ideology and the New South Wales Legislative Council, 1856 72."* PhD thesis, Australian National University, 1974, 30. https://openresearch-repository.anu.edu.au/bitstream/1885/124864/2/b10150663_Connolly_Christopher_Newland.pdf

Curthoys Ann, and Mitchell, Jessie. *Taking Liberty.* Cambridge University Press, 2018.

Dilke, Charles Wentworth, Sir, 1843–1911. *Greater Britain: A Record of Travel in English-Speaking Countries, With Additional Chapters on English Influence in Japan and China, and on Hong Kong and the Straits Settlements,* London: Macmillan and Co., 1907.

Gamboz, Chiara. *"Petitions from Indigenous Australians: Emergence and Negotiations of Indigenous Authorship and Writings."* Unpublished PhD thesis, 2012, 42, downloaded from http://hdl.handle.net/1959.4/52311 in https://unsworks.unsw.edu.au.

Hamilton, Reg. *Colony Strange Origins of One of the Earliest Modern Democracies,* Kent Town, South Australia: Wakefield Press, 2010.

Hasluck, Alexandra, ed. *Audrey Tennyson's Vice-Regal Days.* Canberra: National Library of Australia, 1978.

La Nauze, John. A. *The Making of the Australian Constitution,* Carlton: Melbourne University Press, 1972.

Macaulay, Thomas Babbington. *The Revolution, George Otto Trevalyan, MP, Selections from the Writings of Lord Macauley.* London: Longmans, Green and Co, 1883.

McMinn, Winston. G. *A Constitutional History of Australia.* Melbourne: OUP, 1979.

Melbourne, Alexander. C. V. *Early Constitutional Development in Australia.* St. Lucia: The University of Queensland - Long Pocket Precinct Indooroopilly, QLD 4068. Australia.

Pike, Douglas. *A Paradise of Dissent: South Australia 1829–1857.* Melbourne: Melbourne University Press, 1967

Richardson, Sarah. *"Independence and Deference: A Study of the West Riding Electorate, 1832-1841."* 1995 PhD thesis. https://etheses.whiterose.ac.uk/541/1/uk_bl_ethos_249203.pdf, accessed May 2024. The University of Leeds School of History September, 1995.

Saunders, Kay. *Workers in Bondage: The Origins and Bases of Unfree Labour in Queensland, 1824–1916.* St. Lucia: University of Queensland Press, 1982.

Serle, Geoffrey. *The Golden Age.* Carlton, Melbourne University Press, 1977.

Silvester, Edward, K, ed. *New South Wales Constitution Bill: The Speeches, in the Legislative Council of New South Wales, on the Second Reading of the Bill for Framing a New Constitution for the Colony.* Sydney: Thomas Daniel, 1853.

Smith, Russell. *1850, A Very Good Year in the Colony of South Australia.* Sydney: Shakespeare Head Press, 1973.

Sweetman, Edward. *Australian Constitutional Development.* Melbourne, Macmillan & Co Limited in association with Melbourne University Press, 1925.

Therry, Roger. *Reminiscences of Thirty Years' Residence in New South Wales and Victoria.* Sydney, Sydney University Press, 1974.

Webb, George. H. F. *Debate in the Legislative Council of the Colony of Victoria on the Second Reading of the New Constitution Bill,* Melbourne, Caleb Turner, 14 Swanston Street, 1854.

Weldon, Kevin. *Macquarie Concise Dictionary* (5th ed.). Sydney: Macquarie Dictionary Publishers Pty Ltd, 1999.

Wentworth, William. *A Statistical, Historical and Political Description of the Colony of New South Wales,* London: Printed for G. and W.B. Whittaker, 1819

Woollacott, Angela. *Settler Society in the Australian Colonies.* Oxford, Oxford University Press, 2015.

Articles and Chapters

Curthoys, Ann, and Mitchell Jessie. "The Advent of Self-Government." In *The Cambridge History of Australia*, edited by Alison Bashford and Stuart Macintyre, vol. 1. Cambridge University Press, 2013.

Melleuish, Gregory,. "Daniel Deniehy, Bede Dalley and the Ideal of the Natural Aristocrat in Colonial New South Wales." *Australian Journal of Politics & History* 33, no. 1 (April 2008): 45.

Phillips, John A., and Charles Wetherell. "The Great Reform Act of 1832 and the Political Modernisation of England." *The American Historical Review*, 100, no. 2 (Apr.1993): 411–36.

Scalmer, Sean. "Containing Contention: A Reinterpretation of Democratic Change and Electoral Reform in the Australian colonies." *Australian Historical Studies* 338, (2011): 347.

Legal

'Votes and Proceedings of the Legislative Council', South Australia.
Hansard (UK).
Hansard Volume 1 (Vic.).
Hansard – ACT Legislative Assembly, accessed January 2023
Victorian Constitution 1855
NSW Constitution 1855
South Australian Constitution 1856.
The Electoral Legislation Amendment (Electoral Equality) Act 2021
Wylde v Attorney General of NSW (1948) 78 CLR 224.

Newspapers and other

Sydney Morning Herald.
South Australian Register.
The Southern Australian.
Henry, Parkes. 'Thanksgiving of Workers for British Liberty' (1843).

Websites

Australian Electoral Commission, History of the Indigenous Vote, Electoral milestones for Indigenous Australians – Australian Electoral Commission (aec.gov.au), accessed November 2023.

Opposition to universal suffrage (historyhome.co.uk); accessed May 2024.

Hough, Anna. The 120th anniversary of women's suffrage in Australia, Womens suffrage – Parliament of Australia (aph.gov.au), accessed 6 March 2023.

Parliament.sa.gov.au, The First Parliament. South Australia Achieves Self Government in 1857, accessed December 2023.

https://nla.gov.au:443/tarkine/nla.obj-645021989, accessed March 2023.

sahistoryhub.history.sa.gov.au, Responsible Government, accessed December 2023.

http://eco.canadiana.ca/view/oocihm.32374/2?r=0&s=1, accessed May 2024.

4 Colony leaders fight for and against democracy

Abstract

Opinionated individuals promoting their views within the scope of the British political spectrum were central to the 1850s debates. There were no organised political parties, although there were associations, factions, and tendencies. In each colony there were those who campaigned for more democracy and those who campaigned for less and a parliament more like that of Britain.

In each colony, certain leaders, 'dreamers and schemers,'[1] had an important influence on the development of democracy in the 1850s. There were associations, factions, and tendencies led by such men but no organised political parties. There was certainly 'widespread collective action.'[2]

In NSW, Robert Lowe, a half-blind British barrister, was in NSW for eight years (1842–1850), returned to Britain, and became a member of the House of Commons.[3] He was responsible when back in Britain for persuading the House of Lords to establish a very wide voting rights under the Australian Constitutions Act 1850. This was the Act that empowered two-thirds elected, one-third nominated Legislative Councils in each colony to draft self-governing constitutions for each colony.

Lowe persuaded the House of Lords to make the voting franchise as wide as it was in Britain. The Lords extended the vote to all male owners of freehold worth £100, and to the occupiers of dwellings worth a rental of £10 per annum, halving the £20 threshold set by the House of Commons. Lowe told the Lords that without this amendment 'many rich ex-convicts would have the vote while many decent immigrants' would not.[4] Inflation acted to increase the voting public well beyond what was intended, as most houses were worth at least £10 per annum. Every man aged 21 years or over with a lease or household of the value of £10 or more was entitled to vote.[5]

Hirst sees this as a key reason for our early democracy, while Scalmer emphasises the democratic agitation in the colonies.[6] Lowe promoted democracy, but by itself this was not enough. The 'spirit of democracy was abroad' and was central to what happened.

DOI: 10.4324/9781003490739-5

Figure 4.1 The Right Hon. Robert Lowe, M.P., convinced the British Parliament to establish a wide franchise under the Australia Constitution Act 1850 (NSW member of the Legislative Council and UK Lord Chancellor)

If the colonists and Legislative Councils had not campaigned vigorously, and then drafted and supported democratic constitutions and electoral laws, votes for all men would not have been introduced until later. It was for example delayed in Tasmania and Western Australia despite Robert Lowe. Robert Lowe was a key part of the liberalising tide; he was not that tide by himself before and after the Australian Constitutions Act 1850. He was not responsible for that Act, for example. Democracy was delayed in Britain, and Canada, and other colonies.

Catherine Helen Spence was the first woman to stand as a candidate for office, for the 1897 Federal Constitutional Convention called to consider a federal constitution. She was an influential campaigner for electoral reform and for proportional representation, as well as for votes for women. She was the daughter of David Spence, Clerk of the Adelaide Municipal Council from 1840 to 1843. The Adelaide Council had the first election in the Australian colonies, in August 1840, arguably the first proportional election in the world.[7]

Catherine Spence spoke to the change of attitudes that votes for women required. In October 1905, at a public gathering in Adelaide to celebrate her birthday, she said:

> I am a new woman, and I know it. I mean an awakened woman ... awakened to a sense of capacity and responsibility, not merely to the family and the household, but to the State; to be wise, not for her own selfish interests, but that the world may be glad that she had been born.[8]

Colonial leaders were restrained by libel laws and the threat of social or political ostracism, still threats today, but were still largely left to put their arguments.

The parliamentary under-secretary, John Ball, referred to colonial language as 'violence and occasional rancour.'[9] Robert Lowe and William Wentworth in the NSW Legislative Council and George Kingston and Francis Dutton in the South Australian put independent political ideas which contradicted, vexed, and frustrated the Governors of the day. Even the leaders such as William Wentworth and John Baker responsible for limiting democracy were not part of a Governor's party but rather were an often belligerent opposition in favour of self-government, Whigs rather than Tories. As Sir William Denison Governor of NSW complained in 1855:

> I am tired of the present system which places the Government in the position of a sort of Guy Fawkes, a figure for everyone to throw dirt at.[10]

Notes

1 Frank Bongiorno, *Dreamers and Schemers* (Latrobe University Press, 2022).

2 J Hirst, *The Strange Birth of Colonial Democracy: New South Wales, 1848–1884* (Sydney: Allen & Unwin, 1998); J Hirst, *Freedom on the Fatal Shore* (Carlton: Black Inc, 2008), 210; S Scalmer, "Containing Contention: A Reinterpretation of Democratic Change and Electoral Reform in the Australian Colonies," *Australian Historical Studies* 42, no. 2 (2011): 338.

3 RL Knight, "Lowe, Robert (1811–1892)," In *Australian Dictionary of Biography*, vol. 2 Melbourne: Melbourne University Press, 1967. Biography – Robert Lowe – Australian Dictionary of Biography (anu.edu.au), accessed January 2023.

4 P Cochrane, *Colonial Ambition* (Carlton: Melbourne University Press, 2006), 256.

5 Australian Constitutions Act 1850, s 4.

6 J Hirst, *The Strange Birth of Colonial Democracy: New South Wales, 1848–1884* (Sydney: Allen & Unwin, 1998); J Hirst, *Freedom on the Fatal Shore* (Carlton: Black Inc, 2008), 210; S Scalmer, "Containing Contention: A Reinterpretation of Democratic Change and Electoral Reform in the Australian Colonies," *Australian Historical Studies* 42, no. 3 (2011): 338.

7 S Eade, "Spence, Catherine Helen (1825–1910)," In *Australian Dictionary of Biography*, vol. 6, Melbourne: Melbourne University Press, 1976. Biography – Catherine Helen Spence – Australian Dictionary of Biography (anu.edu.au), accessed January 2023. See also "Election of the First City Council 1840," City of Adelaide website. Election of the first city council 1840 | City of Adelaide; accessed January 2023.

8 S Magarey, "Catherine Helen Spence," SA History Hub, History Trust of South Australia, https://sahistoryhub.history.sa.gov.au/people/catherine-helen-spence, accessed January 2023.
9 P Cochrane, *Colonial Ambition* (Carlton: Melbourne University Press, 2006), 401.
10 Cochrane, *Colonial Ambition*, 2006, 422–23.

Bibliography

Books and Articles

Blackett, John. *History of South Australia*. Adelaide: Hussey & Gillingham, 1911.
Baker, Donald,W.A. "John Dunmore Lang." *Australian Dictionary of Biography*, vol. 2. Melbourne: Melbourne University Press, 1967.
Bongiorno, Frank. *Dreamers and Schemers*. Collingwood VIC, Australia: La Trobe University Press in conjunction with Black Inc, 2022.
Cochrane, Peter. *Colonial Ambition*. Carlton: Melbourne University Press, 2006.
Curthoys, Ann, and Mitchell Jessie. "The Advent of Self-Government." In *The Cambridge History of Australia*, edited by Alison Bashford and Stuart Macintyre, vol. 1. Melbourne, Vic: Cambridge University Press, 2013.
Eade, S. "Spence, Catherine Helen (1825–1910)." *Australian Dictionary of Biography*, vol. 6. Melbourne: Melbourne University Press, 1976.
Hirst, John. *The Strange Birth of Colonial Democracy: New South Wales, 1848–1884*. Sydney: Allen & Unwin, 1998.
Hirst, John. *Freedom on the Fatal Shore*. Carlton: Black Inc, 2008.
Knight, RL. "Lowe, Robert (1811–1892)." In *Australian Dictionary of Biography*, vol. 2. Melbourne: Melbourne University Press, 1967.
Scalmer, S. "Containing Contention: A Reinterpretation of Democratic Change and Electoral Reform in the Australian colonies." *Australian Historical Studies*, 42, no. 3, (2011).

Other

'Votes and Proceedings of the Legislative Council' (SA), 1852.
Australian Constitutions Act 1850.
Election of the first city council 1840', City of Adelaide website. Election of the first city council 1840 | City of Adelaide; accessed January 2023.
Eurekapedia website: Charter of Rights – eurekapedia, which also has a copy of the Charter of Rights, 2020.
Magarey, S. 'Catherine Helen Spence', SA History Hub, History Trust of South Australia, https://sahistoryhub.history.sa.gov.au/people/catherine-helen-spence, accessed January 2023

5 Obstructive Legislative Councils

Abstract

The modern liberal democracies that operate today as Australian States were not the vision of William Wentworth, JLFV 'Alphabet' Foster, and John Baker. However, the obstructive upper houses of parliament they designed lasted well into the 20th century and frustrated more radical governments. The last property qualification for a State upper house was removed in 1973 in South Australia or 1978 in NSW for direct elections introduced.

Introduction

Legislative Councils elected on a property qualification in Victoria and South Australia, and a nominated Legislative Council in NSW, obstructed more radical Government measures until well into the 20th century. Those opposed to democracy during the 1850s debates were unable to delay one man, one vote in the Legislative Assemblies for long, but the price they extracted was obstructive upper houses.

This was the lingering vision of William Wentworth, JLFV ('Alphabet') Foster, and John Baker, the main leaders in the three colonies who fought to limit democracy. The last property qualification was not removed until 1973 in South Australia or direct election provided for in 1978 in NSW.

In NSW and Victoria there was self-government from 1855 but also with short-lived property qualifications on voting rights for the Legislative Assembly.

The nominated upper house of NSW was weaker. The Government of the day could advise the Governor to swamp the Legislative Council with new nominations. There was a mechanism of last resort to resolve disputes between the houses, unlike Victoria and South Australia, where upper houses could simply continue to block legislation.

To understand the limitations on democracy requires an unappealing trek through complicated and varying qualifications developed by the worst sort of quibbling attorneys, but this was typical of Britain and its colonies. In NSW the 1855 constitution provided that a voter had to own land worth £100 or be a

DOI: 10.4324/9781003490739-6

£10 leaseholder to be eligible to vote for the Legislative Assembly.[1] This was changed to one man, one vote in 1858.[2] The 1855 constitution established a nominated not elected Legislative Council.[3]

In Victoria the 1855 constitution required ownership of land worth £2000 or rental £200 to stand for the Legislative Assembly. To vote for the Assembly required ownership of land of £50 or annual rental value of £5.[4] This was changed to one man, one vote in 1857.[5] The constitution required ownership of land worth £5000 or annual value of £500 to stand for the Legislative Council.[6] To vote required ownership of land worth £1000 or annual rental of £100.[7]

Figure 5.1 John Foster, Colonial Secretary, political killer who developed an obstructive Victorian legislative council

In South Australia the 1856 constitution provided for a Legislative Assembly of 36 members elected by 'manhood suffrage,' all men voting, and a Legislative Council of 18 members elected by three classes of property holders: holders of freehold worth £50, leaseholders holding £20 annual value, and tenants of £25 annual rental.[8]

The essentially 18th-century vision behind these limitations on democracy are suggested by William Wentworth's 1853 committee report, which said that the committee wished something analogous to the British Constitution and that it had 'no wish to sow the seeds of a future democracy.' Wentworth thought that 'representation should be based on ... not the mere population ... but should be so proportioned that no one interest shall have a preponderating influence over any other.' In fact but for the Electoral Act 1851, he would have supported a lesser role for Sydney and more for the pastoral industry 'incomparably the largest, the most important interest in the country.' He supported the two-thirds majority requirement in each house before the seat distribution heavily weighted in favour of more conservative country areas could be altered, which was repealed in 1857, two years later.[9]

Radical opposition was unable to organise sufficiently to petition London or stop the 1855 NSW and Victorian constitutions taking effect, unlike in South Australia, where a similar draft constitution was rejected by the Colonial Office after a petition to London organised by George Kingston.

Figure 5.2 William Charles Wentworth, campaigned for self-government and then to restrict democracy

The resulting self-government was almost immediately subject to democratisation of the Legislative Assemblies in NSW and Victoria. In Victoria, the period of the Legislative Assembly was reduced from five to three, and in NSW the two-thirds majority provision was removed. Votes for all men were introduced in separate amendments to the Electoral Acts in 1857 and 1858, respectively.

Turner comments on the pent-up democratic frustrations of the colonists who now suddenly had a means of achieving power although often shut out in the old country:

> Was it surprising that these inexperienced men, who had so suddenly entered upon such a grand heritage, should be impatient to make experiments in political economy which were checked in the motherland by the restricting influences of a thousand years of tradition and precedent?[10]

However, in the three colonies upper houses remained unreformed until the 20th century.

Table 5.1 The development of one person one vote in the Australian colonies and States – South Australia, Victoria, NSW

Australia Self Government Act 1850 – Legislative Council	South Australian Constitution 1856	NSW Constitution 1855	Victorian Constitution 1855	Victorian Electoral Act 1857	NSW Electoral Act 1858
LC vote: land worth £100; leaseholders £10	LA: All men could vote LC vote: land worth £50; leaseholders £20 annual value; tenants £25 annual rental.	LA: land worth £100; leaseholders £10 LC: Nominated by Governor	LA: to stand own land £2000 or rental £200; To vote own land of £50 or annual rental value of £5.[11] LC: to stand own land of £5000 or annual value of £500.[12] To vote own £1000 in land or annual rental of £100.[13]	LA: All men could vote LC: same as 1855	LA: All men could vote LC: same as 1855

The Victorian Legislative Council 1855–1952

In Victoria, the Legislative Council rejected almost 30 bills and 'mutilated' a land bill.[14] Then, when Premier James McCulloch tried to introduce a protective tariff for industry in 1865 by attaching it to an appropriation bill, the Council voted 20 to 5 to 'lay aside' the bill. The premier reacted by using dubious administrative means to finance the government. In November 1865 the premier sent a tariff bill to the Council as a separate bill, which was rejected. McCulloch held an election on the issue and increased his majority.[15] The Council refused to pass his bill and the government resigned. Then McCulloch resumed government and sent the bill to the Council for a third time. In April 1866 a compromise was reached and tariffs were introduced.

Another crisis occurred when the House voted for a pension for Governor Darling, who had supported McCulloch in the matter of raising funds to avoid the Council and had antagonised the Council. In 1867 the House passed an appropriation bill which provided for this pension. But the Council rejected it. The government resigned and was recommissioned when no alternative government could be found. An election was called, and McCulloch was again successful. The British Secretary of State, the Duke of Buckingham, intervened by sending instructions to the Governor, and McCulloch resigned at this inappropriate intervention. A new government survived only a fortnight.

Yet another clash occurred in 1877 when Premier Graham Berry included payment of members of parliament, which had been introduced on a temporary basis, into the appropriations bill. This was rejected by the Council.[16] Berry wanted again to use administrative means to finance payment. In March the Council passed the appropriation bill, and payment of members in a separate bill.

In July 1879 Berry proposed another reform bill providing that appropriation bills would take effect on passage through the Assembly, and other bills would take effect if passed twice by the Assembly although the Council could demand a plebiscite. This failed to pass the Assembly, and at the subsequent election Berry was defeated. He was returned after a second election, and both the Assembly and Council then passed a bill which increased the membership of the Council from 30 to 42, reduced member terms of office from ten years to six and reduced the value of freehold property for members from £2500 to £1000. The qualification for voting had been reduced to £500 in 1869 and was replaced by one which gave the vote to owners of property with a rental value of £10 and to £25 leaseholders. Crises continued until the third quarter of the 20th century.

The Victorian Graham Berry was perhaps the first mass political leader in Victoria and found the Council more than a check on 'hasty' legislation. It prevented an elected Government implementing its programme.[17]

Yet the restrictions of a more conservative and less democratic upper house had enough local support to last until the 1950s–1970s, despite attacks by many including my own relative, Walter Hamilton, then a Labor member of the Victorian Legislative Assembly, who raged against the upper house as a traditional obstructive bastion of the 'upper classes,' like the House of Lords, whose power over money bills was only prevented by the 'deep-rooted traditions brought down from the middle ages.'[18]

The South Australian Legislative Council 1856–1973

The Legislative Council in South Australia, with a lower property qualification for voting, attempted to amend the first appropriations bill after responsible government, which led to a compromise. It could 'suggest' amendments to any money bill except 'that proportion of the Appropriation Bill that provides for the ordinary annual expenses of government.' It could then accept or reject the disputed measure if the Assembly did not accept its suggestions. This was a significant power, as demonstrated in 1876–1879, when it refused to pass loan estimates and when the government rejected its 'suggestion' of a reduction. A government proposal for joint sittings to resolve conflicts was rejected in 1881, and instead an almost unworkable compromise was implemented, under which elections were held if a bill was twice passed by the House of Assembly and twice rejected by the Legislative Council, with a general election intervening.[19]

The Legislative Council of NSW 1855–1978

The nominated Legislative Council of NSW was less of a check, as it was under constant threat of being 'swamped' and may have acted consistent with the British House of Lords, following a practice of concession. It successfully blocked measures in 1858 and the Governor refused to make swamping appointments. He agreed to do so in 1861, and then, criticised for so doing by London, refused in 1873. The Governor's willingness to swamp the Council increased and many nominations were made in the 1880s. The Legislative Council's influence was substantially weakened. The pattern was similar with Queensland's nominated Legislative Council, although the Council there had more influence.[20]

The Legislative Councils linger unreformed until 20th century

The blocking activities of the upper houses did not however lead to such widespread opposition that their less democratic nature became intolerable to the voting public. Those eligible to vote for the Councils continued to support them.

In Britain the House of Lords did not have its blocking powers removed until 1911, and it remains unelected until today. One person one vote was not introduced to the South Australian Legislative Council until 1973, the last Council to be reformed, or 1978 when direction elections were provided in NSW.

Table 5.2 One person, one vote introduced in the Legislative Councils

NSW	1934 by indirect election; 1978 by direct election
Vic	1952
WA	1964
Tas	1968
SA	1973
Qld	n/a: Legislative Council abolished in 1922

Even after these reforms there continued to be unequal electorates, and a weighting towards the country areas, the last one removed in Western Australia in 2021.[21]

No detailed summary of the role played by the Legislative Councils from 1850 until they were reformed has been attempted. On the assumption that the Legislative Councils protected property and the market economy, we should remember that the Australian standard of living was and is founded on the productivity of the market economy.

But not all defence of property was necessarily helpful. The Legislative Councils fought land reform, and nevertheless land reform legislation passed in each colony, which helped ordinary people and economic development and prosperity. Squatters did not dominate politics, as they did in for example South America, to the arguable detriment of South American economic development, which lagged well behind that of the Australian colonies. The Australian colonies resembled the North American not South American colonies in prosperity and democracy. The British supported the new constitutions and helped provide stability.[22]

Second, as well as land reform, the modern 'mixed' economy of progressive taxation, labour laws, health, social welfare, and education systems was developed, mostly in the 20th century despite difficulties in the upper houses. The 1896 wages boards were passed in Victoria but only after a long struggle with the Legislative Council.[23]

Progressive political figures sometimes maintain that more reform should have occurred and would have been beneficial. In Queensland the Legislative Council rejected or amended over 800 bills of the Ryan Labor Government, which eventually succeeded in abolishing the Council in 1922.[24] This also meant that there was less review of legislation of the Coalition Bjelke-Peterson Governments (1968–1987), which progressives often strongly opposed.

The modern approach to Legislative Councils in Australia

The modern approach in Australia is no property qualifications, and equal electorates in State Legislative Councils, as well as harmonising election cycles and other harmonisation measures. This may be the ultimate democratic answer to the long Australian debate about upper houses of parliament unless abolition is supported to enable easier passage of radical legislation of either side of politics.

In some upper houses minor parties or independents of conservative or progressive disposition have the balance of power which are a significant influence on the legislative process, either a frustration or a needed check. The Australian Senate provides the same number of Senators to NSW and Tasmania, despite the vast population differences, and is a 'State's house.' There are a variety of upper houses in other first-world countries.

Notes

1 New South Wales Constitution Act 1855 (UK), clause XI. There are several special additional qualifications in each colony such as holders of mining licences or university degrees. I have omitted them for the sake of brevity. They can be seen in the Annexures.
2 Electoral Reform Act 1858 (NSW), clause 9.
3 New South Wales Constitution Act 1855 (UK), clauses II, III.
4 Victorian Constitution 1855, clause XI.
5 Electoral Act 1857 (Vic), clauses II and III.
6 Victorian Constitution 1855, clause IV.
7 Victorian Constitution 1855, clause V.
8 Constitution Act 1856 (SA), South Australian Constitution 1856, An Act to establish a Constitution for South Australia, and to grant a Civil List to Her Majesty 1856, clauses 6 and 16.
9 A. C. V. Melbourne, *Early Constitutional Development in Australia* (St. Lucia: University of Queensland Press 1963), 400, 404, 426. Clauses XV, XXXVI of the 1855 Constitution.
10 Henry Turner, *A History of the Colony of Victoria*, vol. II (London: Longmans, Green & Co, 1904), 363.
11 Victorian Constitution 1855, clause XI.
12 Victorian Constitution 1855, clause IV.
13 Victorian Constitution 1855, clause V.
14 WG McMinn, *A Constitutional History of Australia* (Melbourne: OUP, 1979), 66.
15 McMinn, *A Constitutional History of Australia*, 1979, 66–67.
16 McMinn, *A Constitutional History of Australia*, 69.
17 Sean Scalmer, *Graham Berry, Democratic Adventurer* (Melbourne: Monash University Publishing, 2020), 207.
18 Reg Hamilton, *Colony*, Adelaide, South Australia: Wakefield Press, 2010, 247.
19 WG McMinn, *A Constitutional History of Australia* (Melbourne: OUP, 1979), 72–73.
20 McMinn, *A Constitutional History of Australia*, 1979, 74–76 NSW, 76 Queensland.
21 Constitutional and Electoral Legislation Amendment (Electoral Equality) Act 2021 (WA).
22 IW McLean, *Why Australia Prospered: The Shifting Sources of Economic Growth* (Princeton, New Jersey: Princeton University Press, 2013), 12, 79.
23 Factories and Shops Act 1896 (Vic)
24 Factsheet_3.20_AbolitionOfTheLegislativeCouncil.pdf (parliament.qld.gov.au), accessed April 2023.

Bibliography

Hamilton, Reg. *Colony*, Kent Town, S. Aust.: Wakefield Press, 2010
McLean, Ian. W. *Why Australia Prospered: The Shifting Sources of Economic Growth.* Princeton, New Jersey: Princeton University Press, 2013.
McMinn, Winston. G. *A Constitutional History of Australia.* Melbourne: OUP, 1979.
Melbourne, Alexander. C. V. *Early Constitutional Development in Australia.* St. Lucia: The University of Queensland - Long Pocket Precinct Indooroopilly, QLD 4068. Australia.
Scalmer, Sean. *Graham Berry, Democratic Adventurer.* Clayton, Monash University Publishing, 2020.

Henry Turner, Henry. *A History of the Colony of Victoria*, vol. II. London: Longmans, Green & Co, 1904.

Factsheet_3.20_AbolitionOfTheLegislativeCouncil.pdf (parliament.qld.gov.au), accessed April 2023

Constitution Act 1856 (SA), South Australian Constitution 1856, An Act to establish a Constitution for South Australia, and to grant a Civil List to Her Majesty 1856.

New South Wales Constitution Act 1855 (UK).

Victorian Constitution Act 1855.

Constitutional and Electoral Legislation Amendment (Electoral Equality) Act 2021 (WA).

Electoral Reform Act 1858 (NSW).

Electoral Act 1857 (Vic).

Factories and Shops Act 1896 (Vic)

6   New South Wales

The 18th-century colony

Abstract

In the 1853 Legislative Council debates, William Wentworth successfully proposed a nominated Legislative Council in full knowledge it could be controlled by threats of new appointments, 'swamping.' He successfully proposed an elected Legislative Assembly with a limited property qualification for voting, maintaining the weighting of seats towards more conservative country areas, and a requirement of a two-thirds majority to change the distribution. However only two years later liberals increased their share of the Legislative Assembly in the 1856 elections. 'Slippery' Charles Cowper replaced the limited property qualification for the Legislative Assembly with votes for all men. The nominated Legislative Council continued until 1934. The two-thirds provision was repealed.

Civil society develops in the prison colony of New South Wales

The development of democratic constitutions in the three more radical colonies was not a simple step from the Durham Report of 1839 and the Australian Constitutions Act 1850 (UK) to giving all men the vote. Democracy was not simply conferred by the British. There was a long struggle in the Legislative Councils about the form that self-government should take and William Wentworth and others sought restrictions on democracy and a Whig constitution in which property was fully represented in parliament.

In any event the Durham report itself was the result of a difficult political process after the Canadian loyalist insurrection of 1835. The 1850 Act was the result of campaigns from NSW colonists, including those who wanted to separate from NSW and become Victoria. Political campaigns and struggles led to the new liberal democracies.

NSW, the original British colony on the Australian continent, had the longest history. It was originally a prison colony of convicts, only gradually liberalising into a colony of the more usual kind. In 1808, the army deposed Governor Bligh after he tried to interfere with their conduct of the rum trade, which operated as an early form of currency. This was the only successful

DOI: 10.4324/9781003490739-7

armed takeover of government in Australian history and became known as the rum rebellion.

NSW was particularly influential. Tasmania (1835), Victoria (1851) and Queensland (1859) were part of NSW and then separated from it. South Australia and Western Australia were not part of NSW but operated under separate legislation.

The Legislative Council in NSW was established in 1923[1] to consist of five to seven members, all appointed, and only the Governor could initiate legislation. It first met in 1824, and until 1838, its proceedings were secret although apparently there were leaks to the free press.[2] In 1828 it was expanded to 7 official and 7 non-official members and in 1842[3] was expanded to 36 members, 12 nominated and 24 elected. This was 'first past the post' voting of the man with the most votes as nearly all elections in colonial Australia were, except for the October 1840 election of the Adelaide City Council, which was a form of proportional representation, arguably the first use in the world.[4] No second and third preferences were distributed as they are now.

The 1850s debates were part of a long series of campaigns for the liberalisation of the colony including a colonist petition in 1819 signed by over 1,200 persons for trial by jury rather than military courts in 1819, and an assertion of the inalienable rights of Englishmen to have meetings and draw up petitions. There was another petition in 1827 for 'Trial by Jury and of Representative Government,' a second petition in 1830, a third petition in 1833, another petition in 1835, the Buller-Macarthur draft constitution of 1838, which was rejected by parliament in 1839, Judge Burton's scheme for representative government in 1839, and much else elaborated by Sweetman and others.[5] The right to petition came from the Bill of Rights 1689 (UK), part of the Glorious Revolution when the Catholic King James II was deposed.

Nominated upper houses had been used in British colonies for centuries and were not unusual. What was new was that the taint of convictism was no longer a bar to representative institutions or voting, subject to a property qualification. In bringing forward the 1842 Act,[6] the British parliament rejected the example of Canada. The Canada Act 1791 debarred emancipists from voting, a position supported by the 'exclusives' in NSW such as John Macarthur and opposed by William Wentworth in his 1819 plan for representative government.[7]

Democratisation defeated the 'squatters,' a term used to describe those who rode out of Sydney and other towns and set up vast sheep and cattle stations on crown land, without legal sanction, and other large landowners. They wished to retain their key role in or domination of politics, retain transportation of convicts and their monopoly of pastoral leases. This would have led to the Argentinian 'road not taken' of much lesser living standards is one view.[8]

The protection of property and a functioning economy were however fundamental to the ideas of the 1850s debates. While the new parliaments had control of Crown lands, and later enacted land reform, this legislation was measured. Land reform did not, as such reform has been done elsewhere and as Macauley and others warned would happen, bring those industries to a halt in an explosion of revolutionary violence. Australia thrived and continued to 'ride on the sheep's back.' Wool was Australia's main export from the 1820s to the 1950s, except for the 1850s–1860s when gold was more important.[9] Democratisation did not damage the developing prosperity but helped it.

Electioneering 1842–1856

The electorate was mostly literate with a 58 per cent literacy rate in 1858 in the Australian colonies if these early statistics are accurate (compared to 80 per cent in 1901).[10] Electioneering was nevertheless often as turbulent as it was in Britain, a party and a riot. There was no secret ballot and votes were cast in public, with resulting commentary and abuse. There was bribery, sometimes in the form of the beer distributed to potential supporters by Captain Hall in Adelaide in the 1851 elections. There was also violence. In 1848 in Sydney rioters burnt polling booths and liberated prisoners from a watch-house. In South Australia in 1851 'pugnacious Irish-men' threatened, and 'ragamuffins' used 'bludgeons' to cause 'serious injury,' nomination day was a 'mere day of riot.'[11] This was the mob that threatened civil disorder and property feared by Macauley and others.

In NSW radicals were initially successful at the municipal level. The first municipal elections for the Sydney Municipal Council were held in 1842 (the second election in the Australian colonies after the Adelaide Municipal election in 1840) and trades delegates and radical intellectuals mobilising ward by ward and managed to elect tradesmen and shopkeepers of the city in preference to gentlemen.[12] They were repeatedly successful between 1848 and 1855. In the 1850 municipal elections for the Corporation of Sydney, the radicals supported six Councillors, holding public meetings chaired by Robert Campbell to choose the candidates, and setting up a committee. Three on their ticket were elected and a further one was a member of a radical organisation.[13]

The Legislative Council became partly elected pursuant to the Constitution Act 1842 (UK). Two-thirds of the Legislative Council members were elected and one-third nominated by the Governor.

Table 6.1 Voting eligibility NSW 1842–1856

Men £200 free-hold or £20 householders	1842	Constitution Act 1842 (UK)
Men £100 free-hold, £10 householders, three-year lease of £10, or depasturing license, five-year term	1850	Australia Constitutions Act 1850 (UK)
Men £100 land or £10 leaseholder – L. Assembly; Nominated – L. Council	1855	New South Wales Constitution Act 1855 (UK)
Men over 21 – L. Assembly Nominated – L. Council	1858	Electoral Reform Act 1858 (NSW)

In NSW there were over one hundred public meetings in support of de-mocracy and the election of democracy-minded candidates between 1848 and 1850.[14] Small associations were formed with Chartist aims with Chartist and anti-Corn Law League organisations 'vaguely taken as models,' which 'followed the traditional pattern of getting up petitions and giving candidates some support in elections.'[15]

The Australian League of 1850 was launched by the Reverend Lang, who demanded votes for all men, vote by ballot and equal electoral districts, and federation of the colonies. His league soon had little support.[16]

A committee of tradesmen, shopkeepers and at least one trades delegate persuaded Robert Lowe to run for Sydney. They were successful with Lowe elected in second place behind Wentworth using the ward-by-ward mobilising that radicals had been promoting since 1842. The Committee to elect Lowe transformed itself into the Constitutional Association, and Edward Hawskley began publishing the Peoples Advocate and New South Wales Vindicator, the main voice of democratic politics until 1856. Henry Parkes was Secretary of the Committee and said that the election of Lowe was the birthday of Austral-ian democracy.[17]

Radical newspapers and associations developed. Henry Parkes was a Chartist and when news of the great Chartist meeting of 10 April 1848 on Kennington Common reached Australia, Parkes and the Constitutional Asso-ciation rejoiced and welcomed it as consistent with their aims for New South Wales.[18]

The NSW Constitutional Association of 1848 was set up. It supported votes for all men, the secret ballot and more frequent elections, and radical land reform.[19] It faded away in 1849 replaced by the more popular anti-trans-portation league.

The Political Association was set up to attack the 1851 Electoral Act and for the 1851 general election, to prevent the blocking of democracy. It at-tacked squatters in 'bitter terms,' and then lost support. Sydney seats had four members out of 36 or 11 per cent, with a Sydney member representing 13,000 people and pastoral electorates 3,300 people. At the 1851 election, the radical Hawksley suggested that three candidates 'of the liberal party' stand for the three-member seat of Sydney and this was taken up by the Political Association. These were Lang, Lamb and Cowper. A Citizens Gen-eral Election Committee was set up to coordinate their campaigns, although they also each kept separate committees. Lang was first in the poll, Lamb second and Wentworth third, but Cowper won a seat elsewhere with 'liberal' support.

Despite intense liberal and radical activity both NSW and Victoria pro-duced Council majorities at the 1851 and 1853 (Victorian) elections that did not support votes for all men and the secret ballot and did not represent popu-lar opinion, unlike more radical South Australia.

The NSW Legislative Council was dominated by William Wentworth, who came last out of three in his seat of Sydney at the 1951 election because he opposed votes for all men and 'the spirit of democracy abroad,' as he called it. Overall of the 36 elected members in NSW in 1851, 11 came from the towns and boroughs, and only 4 from radical Sydney, 17 from the settled counties, and 8 from the pastoral districts. The result was that 'the exclusive landed interest had an overwhelming majority,' and 'popular opinion was not an important influence.'[20]

The 1853 debates and 1855 constitution carefully restricting democracy were the obvious result of such a Council.

Figure 6.1 Stuart A. Donaldson, first Premier of New South Wales. Ca 1860

Figure 6.2 William Charles Wentworth, campaigned for self-government and then to restrict democracy

Figure 6.3 Sir Henry Parkes, Chartist, and later leader of Federation in 1901

Figure 6.4 Mr. Charles Cowper (1807–1875), Premier of NSW, gave all men the vote in 1858

1853 NSW debates

On 20 May 1853 the two-thirds elected one third nominated Legislative Council established a committee to develop a new constitution, chaired by William Wentworth and with a conservative majority. The committee reported on 28 July 1853 and recommended a new colonial aristocracy for the upper house based on that in French Quebec:

> Your committee are not prepared to recommend the introduction into this colony of a right by descent to a seat in the Upper House; but are of opinion that the creation of hereditary titles, leaving it to the option of the crown to annex the title of the first Patentee a seat for life in such house, and conferring on the original Patentees and their descendants inheritors of their titles a power to elect a certain number of their order to form, in conjunction with the original Patentees then living, the Upper House of Parliament, would be a great improvement upon any form of Legislative Council hitherto tried or recommended in any British colony. They conceive that an Upper House framed on this principle, whilst it would be free from

the objections which have been urged against the House of Lords, on the ground of the hereditary right of legislation which they exercise, would lay the foundation of an aristocracy, which, from their fortune, birth, leisure, and the superior education these advantages would superinduce, would soon supply elements for the formation of an Upper House, modelled, as far as circumstances will admit, upon the analogies of the British Constitution. Such a house will be a close imitation of the elective portion of the House of Lords, which is supplied from the Irish and Scotch peerage; nor is it the least of the advantages which would arise from the creation of a titled order, that it would necessarily form one of the strongest inducements not only to respectable families to remain in this colony, but to the upper classes of the United Kingdom and other countries who are desirous to emigrate, to choose it for their future abode.[21]

Before he abandoned the proposal, Wentworth justified his new colonial aristocracy by referring to the Quebec Act, and to the Charter of the Colony of Maryland in North America, which gave Lord Baltimore the power to create a hereditary peerage.[22]

Wentworth's 1853 committee report said it wished something analogous to the British Constitution and that it had 'no wish to sow the seeds of a future democracy.' Wentworth thought that 'representation should be based on … not the mere population … but should be so proportioned that no one interest shall have a preponderating influence over any other.' He supported the two-thirds majority requirement to change the constitution which was repealed in 1857 two years later.[23]

Wentworth justified his rejection of democracy in his second reading speech by referring at length to criticisms made of American democracy by Alexis de Tocqueville, including 'that it excludes from power the upper and best educated classes, and throws the government of the country completely into the hands of the lower classes,[24] the despotism of the majority,[25] abuse of power, anarchy, and tendency towards corruption.[26] He also quoted John Calhoun. He concluded his second reading speech dramatically: 'What do I want? Do I want the American constitution, or do I want the constitution of England?'[27]

Wentworth argued for the existing distribution of seats embodied in the Electoral Act 1851:[28]

The distribution it involves of the representation of the town population is, I think, amply sufficient. But I cannot see how we could consistently have taken any other course than that which the committee has adopted. So long as the Electoral Act of 1851 remained on the statute book, we have no right to depart from the principle of that bill. I repeat, I took an active part in that bill, and from the experience we have had of its working, I am convinced it was one of the wisest measures the Legislature have ever passed. (Cheers.)

It has worked most beneficially; it has proved that it was quite fitted to insure a fair representation of all the interests of the country in the House. The principle of providing the representative faculty contained in that bill has given us a Legislature fitted, and with full power and authority from the country to frame a constitution for the colony.

Mr. Darvall replied in opposition, pointing out that John Calhoun 'was the proprietor of large slave plantations,'[29] and pointing out that:[30]

The honourable gentleman was much mistaken, if he supposed that anybody of Englishmen would consent to constitute a minority as a superior or privileged race with hereditary legislative power. It would be an odious effort of tyranny; not endured by anyone who could resist it, but laughed at from one end of the world to another. The honourable gentleman, in dwelling so long on charters conferred by bad kings, altogether lost sight of the earlier Anglo-Saxon institutions. If he would refer to them, he would find, that in matters of local detail, the principles of election and of double election were pursued, even in the smallest country matters, beginning with tithings and hundreds, and providing for the election of freemen, liverymen, aldermen, and so on. These elective institutions have been entirely overlooked, and attention was directed to the case of the people driven out of their country by tyranny, and obliged to yield to fresh tyranny, in the land of their settlement, until they shook the intolerable yoke from off their necks.

He concluded by referring to general democratic tendencies that should be followed:

I would, however, ask what is the object of representation at all? Who made Legislatures? Who gave to legislatures the powers which they exercise? Are not all Legislatures supposed to represent the people? I do not mean to say that mere numbers should alone be taken into account, but when my honourable friend goes so far as to say that Sydney does not require to be represented, I am surprised that his perverted line of reasoning did not lead him to go further and say that it should not be represented because it contained so many people. (Hear, and laughter.) …

   I would ask if the honourable member had kept in view the 'greatest happiness of the greatest number.' Now, if that doctrine is to be considered sound, it follows that representation should be in fair proportion to population wherever the capacity for self-government is admitted. While I do not go so far as to say that particular classes and interests should not be represented, I would ask, is it reasonable or not to say, that the largest constituency in the colony should be disfranchised, because it is the seat of Government? My honourable friend's fallacies are, in fact, without end. (Hear, hear, and disapprobation.)[31]

Mr. Darvall tried to claim that an elected upper house would be consistent with retaining the monarchy,[32] leading Wentworth to say that[33] 'the inevitable tendency of an elective Upper Chamber, in combination with an elective Chamber of Representatives below, is to sever the connection with the mother country.' John Bayley Darvall was a leader who sought an elected upper house and other democratisation measures such as more equal electorates which were weighted in favour of the conservative country.

Mr. Martin was concerned about the potential for mob rule and referred to the US Senate as showing that:

> They knew the nature of popular assemblies, and that the immediate dependence of their members upon their constituents render them peculiarly open to be influenced by every change of popular opinion, and that there is a propensity in all numerous assemblies to yield to sudden impulses, and be led by party feeling, and under the influence of factious leaders into intemperate resolutions. In all such large assemblies it is easy for mere agitators to obtain a paramount control. Consequently, they thought it advisable to establish a less numerous and more dignified body; less liable than the other to dangerous influences, either from within or without.[34]

Mr. Martin accused Mr. Darvall of being a Chartist radical supporting equal districts and universal suffrage:

> If we are to place any reliance upon the opinions of the Radicals and Chartists, and admirers of the American Constitution, we should adopt the principle of equal electoral districts and universal suffrage. This view indeed is not confined to the Radicals and the Chartists. I find that it is adopted by the honourable and learned member for Cumberland, who, in his speech last night, laid down the doctrine that 'every man who breathes the air has a right to share in legislation, either personally or by representative.'[35]

Mr. Darvall said 'I never stated anything of the sort.'[36]
Mr. Martin responded[37]:

> The honourable and learned gentleman certainly did say this – 'Why should any man give rights in which he is not to share.' Now, if this is not advocating universal suffrage, I am at a loss to know what is. Those who are in favour of universal suffrage have one great difficulty to get over before they can expect their ideas to be received with any favour by persons of real intelligence. They must establish the right to have a direct voice in the choice of representatives to be one of the original inherent rights of man. Unless they can make this out clearly and indisputably they must

fail to establish their case, and the franchise must be regulated upon some principle of expediency by those in whose hands the chief power may happen to be placed. Now, what are the natural rights of man? He has a right to personal liberty – he has a right to personal security – he has a right to the enjoyment of his property – i.e. has a right to do as he likes, so long as by so doing he does not trespass on the rights, or interfere with the liberty of others. Governments are established to protect and secure those rights, and for no other purpose. If human nature were perfect – if all men would spontaneously abstain from interfering with each other's rights – government would then be unnecessary. But the fallibility and perversity of human nature are such, that men will not respect each other's rights unless they are coerced by some superior power. Government, therefore, is a matter of necessity. And it follows from this that all that has to be considered in the formation of a government is, – in what way the natural rights of man can be best protected. Whatever government is best calculated to protect those rights; that is unquestionably the best form of government – no matter whether it be based on universal suffrage, or limited suffrage, or no suffrage at all. The rights of suffrage are a means, and not an end; and they have been so regarded by every eminent man who has entered upon the consideration of this question. The right to elect representatives is no original right of man, because it is a thing unknown to man, except in civil society. It arose from the necessity of imposing checks upon those entrusted with the preservation of man's rights, and it can be carried no further than the exigency of the case requires. There is no record in history to show us how society was first organized. How the fabric of government was first raised is a matter of pure speculation. It cannot be supposed that any number of persons met together, and formed themselves into a community at once. It is more reasonable to imagine that the first regular government had its origin in a usurpation – in a despotism wherein a single individual, taking advantage of some superiority displayed by him in war or commotion of some kind, seized upon the supreme authority. There can be little reason to doubt that such was the origin of government. Experience, however, would soon teach the people under such a rule, that although one despot might be wise and beneficent, his successor might be the reverse – that the same government, which in the hands of one man might be the best, in the hands of another might become the worst. Thus constitutional checks of some kind would come to be sought for, and obtained, one by one, not as rights, but as necessities for the preservation of rights.

Mr. Macarthur said[38] that Mr. Calhoun demonstrated that American universal suffrage led to 'this wholesale system of corruption …' He concluded by stating that 'Reason and England will prevail against Democracy and America.'[39]

The Colonial secretary said that the franchise would be extended and self-government including control of crown lands introduced:[40]

The next important principle of the Bill is the extension of the franchise, and this also is one which should not be passed over. By this extension a great advantage will be afforded, seeing that it will give to many educated and deserving persons the right to vote, a new and important feature in the measure, which I believe will be received with favour by the community. The next point is the most important in the whole Bill, being, as it is, the very keystone of the constitution. It secures to the representatives the full and uncontrolled management of all the revenues of the colony, whether territorial or otherwise, including royalties of every kind. (Cheers.) The ramifications into which this power must extend penetrate through the whole constitution. It is a power which must give the Legislature the complete control of the government. (Great cheers.) It is the way in which responsible government must be introduced, and under such a power responsible government can alone exist. It is useless to say, as some honourable members in the House, and some people out of the house do, that the time for responsible government has not yet come, and that the colony is not yet fitted for it but, however, I do not for one moment disguise the fact from myself, that as soon as this power is granted, responsible government must take place; and my honourable colleagues in the government are as well assured of this as I am myself.

Mr. Nichols said:[41]

I must again express my concurrence with my friend Sam Slick, who thus describes the minister's toast – 'May our Government never degenerate into a mob, nor our mobs grow strong enough to become our Government.' (Loud and long continued cheers.)

Sam Slick was a character in satirical books written about England and elsewhere by the Canadian author Thomas Chandler Haliburton.
Mr. Parker said:[42]

The whole scope of the arguments in the house have been as between the British Constitution and other Constitutions.

Mr. Berry summarised the arguments in the house as:[43]

With reference to the great point, the institution of two Houses of parliament, it appears that all parties are agreed: but with this wide difference – the mode of returning the members. That party which supports the Bill before the Council advocate a nominee Upper, and an elective Lower Chamber. The opponents of the Bill contend that both Chambers should

be elective. Then the first party are stanch advocates for monarchical principles; the second vehement clamorers for republicanism. (Loud cheers.)

Mr. Darvall clarified his position after attacks by Wentworth and others:[44]

> What I meant to say was this: no doubt the time may come – at all events
> those who most heartily desire the longest adherence to our connection
> with Great Britain must admit that the time may come when a severance
> of that connection must take place. I say, then, that the expectation of a
> transition to a limited monarchy, without a previous course of bloodshed
> and revolution, is unwarranted by history, and that so long as we continue
> under a monarchical form of government an elective Legislature will be
> more conducive to that continuance, and when the time of separation from
> the parent state does come it will render the separation easier.

Finally, Mr. Wentworth said that the question he wanted approved by the
house was the following:

> the sole principle I wish to have affirmed by the second reading is, that
> there shall be two Houses of Parliament, an Upper and a lower House, and
> that whether the upper House is to be elective or nominated is to remain
> an open question until we shall receive an expression of opinion from the
> different districts of the country on that subject; and that this important
> part of this measure shall only be determined when the House goes into a
> committee of the whole house...

The Legislative Council passed that resolution 33 Ayes to 8 Noes.[45]

Wentworth and most others saw his Constitution Bill as a working out of
the British Constitution in Australia. The Postmaster-General said that the Bill
was a close approximation of the British Constitution, as close as we can devise.[46] Mr. Parker said[47] that he wanted to live under the British Constitution,
not that of another country.[48] Wentworth said[49] that the people of this country
have a right to the British Constitution not more and not to a Yankee Constitution of an elective Upper Chamber.

Wentworth quoted Alexander Pope on the 'beautiful mixture of antagonis-
tic elements which it [the British Constitution] contains':[50]

> Till jarring interests of themselves create
> The according music of a well-mixed State

His final address included other poetic flourishes:[51]

> And Australasia float, with flag unfurled,
> A New Britannia in another world!
> [Enthusiastic cheering, the gallery joining in the applause]

The recommendation of a colonial aristocracy and upper house composed of one came as a 'surprise' to other members as it had been opposed by at least three members of the committee, and others said the hereditary clauses were 'dispensable.' It was then opposed by leading conservatives such as Manning, Douglas and the editors of the Sydney Morning Herald. It was ridiculed by Daniel Deniehy and many others.[52]

Wentworth then proposed instead a wholly nominated upper house whose members were not to possess titles,[53] in full awareness that it could be 'swamped.' Arguments advanced by conservatives in favour of a nominated upper house included that an elected one was a 'disloyal' preference for American institutions, but their reasons may not have been entirely clear.[54]

Other liberals such as Robert Lowe supported a nominated upper house because 'the opinions of such a house would not carry much weight; not half so much as that of the representatives of the people.'[55]

A nominated upper house was established in NSW. The Legislative Assembly was established with a property qualification. A voter had to own land worth £100 or be a £10 leaseholder to be eligible to vote. Electorates were unequal in size and weighted against the city and towards the country.

The New South Wales Constitution Act 1855 (UK) received the Royal Assent on 16 July. The new parliament sat for the first time on 22 May 1856. The 'conservative/liberal' Stuart Donaldson became the first Premier under responsible government.

NSW gives all men the vote: 1858

The limited democracy of William Wentworth and his allies did not last. Premier Charles ('Slippery Charlie') Cowper's Electoral Reform Act 1858 introduced one man, one vote for the Legislative Assembly during his second ministry, along with the secret ballot and a more equal distribution of seats according to population. His government was the fourth since responsible self-government began in 1856.

In NSW Governor Denison like many others calculated that the Legislative Assembly after the 1856 election consisted of about 34 conservatives and 20 'Liberals or Republicans,'[56] and after the election in 1858, only 1 of 23 liberals who stood again were defeated while of the 15 conservatives who stood again only 8 were successful. Cowper secured the support of the liberals by promising to revise the 1851 Electoral Act and land reform.[57]

After the 1858 election Cowper had the support of most urban electorates while most pastoral electorates (16) supported the opposition Donaldson and Parker, although Cowper had the support of 9 pastoral electorates, a rough liberal/conservative divide very different to the 33/8 divide on Wentworth's second reading speech in 1853.[58] Parliament was becoming reconciled with popular opinion.

Mr. Cowper gave a speech which was at best limited in nature and was criticised by Mr. Macleay as 'meagre' for such a major bill. Mr. Cowper said that in discussing the Constitution Bill he had argued for a system of representation 'based on population, not property,' the principle of this bill as well. He said that the government was not at that time prepared to prohibit the introduction of Chinese into the country. He thought that the law ought not actually prohibit the Chinese from voting. He reviewed in detail the distribution of voters for each seat, highlighting the large differences. He supported a reallocation of seats by population, including a large increase in the seats in Sydney.[59]

Mr. Donaldson (Leader of the Opposition) opposed the bill as promising despotism like the French revolution and spoke in support of a property qualification. The *Sydney Morning Herald* reported that Donaldson:[60]

> considered the franchise ought to depend upon three conditions education, residence, and property of the three absolutely, but two out of the three were demanded by every statesman who had thought it right to speak on the subject. He did not advocate any greater right for the man of property in the electoral district in which he resided, than for the man of no property, provided he possessed the qualifications of residence and intelligence, and he contended the normal condition of the countries, was a proof that they ought not to go to any theory to find out how to ensure the greatest good to the greatest number. There was nothing absolutely certain, but beginning with a negative, he entirely denied the 'Rights of Man' by Tom Paine. (Hear, hear, and laughter.)

Mr. Donaldson said that the bill:[61]

> was a revolution, not a reform. The bill proposed to give a power which he defied hon. members to produce a parallel to in the whole civilised world. There were plenty of examples of despotic governments yielding to popular influences. They could produce examples of despotic governments yielding to revolution for instance, France had given way by reason of a revolution. But what was the result that they had a more despotic government than they had when Louis XVI was deposed.

He said that the bill would:

> create a Legislative Assembly that had the absolute power of making the Constitution of the country. The Legislative Assembly would then be a convention in every sense of the word, and as dangerous and as damnable as that of 1789 as destructive of property and as destructive of liberty. That was his belief, and as long as he expressed what he believed to be the truth,

he would not hesitate to say what he thought. They were about to create a convention in the country with no check whatever upon its democratic tendencies.

Mr. Campbell (Colonial Treasurer) gave a more wide-ranging and reasoned speech than the premier supporting the bill:

> Was it not a bill that the people of England had been agitating for during the last fifteen hundred years in fact, ever since he was a boy. (Roars of laughter). It involved the grand principle of representation according to population – a principle which the ancient Saxons tried hard to work out. And would anybody tell him that the ancient Saxons were revolutionary? He denied it. (Laughter.) The simple object of the bill was to give every honest man a vote; and when he came to consider the dispersion of population, he was at a loss to perceive how the representation could have been more equitably apportioned than it was in the bill. He could not possibly see that nine members were too many for a city like Sydney, containing as it did 80,000 souls, and treasure in the coffers of the bank to the extent of about £6,000,000 sterling. He was also in favour of vote by ballot, as proposed in the bill, because he believed it was the safest protection they could afford the poor against the intimidation of the rich.[62]

He said that:

> The English people were now demanding from the House of Commons a still further increase of the popular representation of the country, there was little reason to complain that the present bill gave undue influence to the democracy of this colony. If this was the case in England, where existed an ancient aristocracy, an influential squirearchy, and a great monied interest, how much more ought it to be the case in a colony where the whole population was democratic. There was nothing in the social state of a rising colony like this that should prevent or control a democracy from exercising that self directing and self-vindicating spirit which they saw everywhere the essential attribute of democracy. It was to that principle that the colony must look for what was most desirable in social' equalities, and it must there look for that protection and power which would enable it to grow so as to obtain the status of a nation …. Here, comparatively speaking, all were upon a level. To prove, that it was only necessary to look round that House, and it would be at once seen how limited was the exception to the rule, that the House was composed of men who had risen through their own industry from the ranks of the people. [Hear, hear]. In principle, this country was essentially democratic, and the difference of grade, so far as it went amongst us, would be laughed at by men in the mother country. They were bound to establish all their institutions in accordance with the spirit of the country.

He supported goldminers having the vote:

> The miner's right was an authority from the Government of the country to dig for gold, for which right he paid a license fee of six months, and the possession of this right was to his mind as substantial a qualification as a mere residency of six months. It appeared unnecessary, unjust, and unreasonable to deprive this valuable class of the community of their political rights, simply because they were gold diggers.

Mr. Macleay criticised the 'meagre' speech of Premier Cowper as unprecedented for a major bill.

Mr. Forster said he supported the principle of equality but there were exceptions for the rural sectors:

> If they were all equal as individual electors, which he believed was an indisputable maxim, then he maintained they should have equal influence in the representation of the country. Because, if any individual or number of individuals were prevented from giving due weight to the exercise of their equal rights, through being mixed up in a large aggregate population, then the number so deprived must necessarily sustain a degree of injustice, and consequently this showed that the population basis was the correct principle upon which any electoral measure should be framed. (Hear, hear.) At the same time, he was not prepared to apply this principle strictly, especially in the interior, where the population was scattered and disunited. (Hear, hear.) There were many cases in his opinion, in which the circumstances of the rural population warranted a departure from the principle, although he admitted that generally it was the only correct one.

Mr. Hay said that the Bill went too far:

> The principle on which he went was this: in all organic changes go step by step, and make well sure that the steps are in the right direction. It was on this account he objected to such a revolutionary measure as that introduced in the present bill. The bill had been blamed as a revolutionary measure.[63]

He said that:

> He had a great objection to the disconnection of property from the elective franchise. He, for his own part, believed that property was the grand basis of civilization, and he believed if property had not its full representation they would go back to what would be a savage state.

Mr. Arnold said that the Bill would give rural men the vote, and city men already had the vote:

This manhood suffrage seems to have been universally described by hon. members opposite as a concession to the prejudices of mobs in towns; but he denied that such was the case. What was the fact? Why, out of every hundred men in Sydney fully ninety-five were represented under the present law whilst in the country, at present, not more than fourteen out of a hundred had the franchise. Thus, then, manhood suffrage was a concession to the hardworking man of the interior, to allow him to take a part in the business of the country, and not one made to the un-thinking mobs of towns.[64]

The bill passed but only after conflict with the conservative-dominated Legislative Council, which substituted for votes for all resident men eligibility requirements of paying a rent of £5 per annum, or possessing, for a period of six months prior to the election, the sum of £100 in a bank. The Legislative Assembly rejected the amendment by 19 votes to 17, and the Legislative Council then conceded votes for all men. It therefore avoided a debate about whether to 'swamp' the Council to get the Bill passed. In Connolly's view the Governor would almost certainly have demanded a dissolution and election before consenting to swamp the Council.[65]

The Council conceded the secret ballot. Deas Thomson said it was a necessary safeguard against working-class intimidation of those of their number who voted for conservative candidates: 'No labouring man would dare to vote against his class. If he did he would become a pariah and an outcast.'[66]

The Council succeeded in obtaining an increase in residency qualifications for foreigners before they could become members of the Assembly from three years to five years of the period of residence. Seats were increased from 54 to 80 plus a seat for Queensland University (reduced to 72 when Queensland separated in 1858).[67]

Of all the Government Ministry John Robertson (Secretary for Lands and Works) was a major support to the Bill and had been a longstanding campaigner for votes for all men, the secret ballot, more equal electorates, for an end to State aid for religion, and against the British Constitution as aristocratic and largely inapplicable to colonial conditions.[68]

Notes

1 The New South Wales Act 1823 (UK).
2 Edward Sweetman, *Australian Constitutional Development* (Melbourne: Macmillan & Co Limited in association with Melbourne University Press, 1925), 51–53.
3 Constitution Act 1842 (UK).

4 John Keane, *The Life and Death of Democracy* (Simon & Schuster UK Ltd, 2009), 520.

5 Edward Sweetman, *Australian Constitutional Development* (Melbourne: Macmillan & Co Limited in association with Melbourne University Press, 1925), xxvii–xxx, 49.

6 Constitution Act 1842 (UK).

7 Edward Sweetman, *Australian Constitutional Development* (Melbourne: Macmillan & Co Limited in association with Melbourne University Press), 159.

8 IW McLean, *Why Australia Prospered: The Shifting Sources of Economic Growth* (Princeton: Princeton University Press, 2013), 67, 76–80.

9 McLean, *Why Australia Prospered: The Shifting Sources of Economic Growth*, 2013, 54.

10 Commonwealth Bureau of Census and Statistics, Official Yearbook of the Commonwealth of Australia No. 1, McCarron: Bird & Co.,1908.

11 S Scalmer, "Containing Contention: A Reinterpretation of Democratic Change and Electoral Reform in the Australian colonies," *Australian Historical Studies* 42, no. 3 (2011): 338, 340–44.

12 Terence Irving, The Southern Tree of Liberty Explained, 2015, 12, https://marxistleftreview.org/articles/the-southern-tree-of-liberty-explained/, Marxist Left Review | 'The Southern Tree of Liberty' explained, accessed May 2024.

13 Terry Irving, Southern Tree of Liberty, 189.

14 Loveday, Parliamentary factions, 1966, 21.

15 Loveday, Parliamentary factions, 1966, 21.

16 Loveday, Parliamentary factions, 1966, 19–20.

17 Terry Irving, Southern Tree of Liberty, 175.

18 P Cochrane, *Colonial Ambition* (Carlton: Melbourne University Press, 2006), 198.

19 A Curthoys and J Mitchell, "The Advent of Self-Government," in *The Cambridge History of Australia*, vol. 1, ed. A Bashford and S Macintyre (London: Cambridge University Press, 2013), 155.

20 A.C.V. Melbourne, *Early Constitutional Development in Australia* (University of Queensland Press, 1963), 382.

21 Silvester, NSW Legislative Council debates, 1853, 2. Catalog Record: New South Wales constitution bill; the | HathiTrust Digital Library, accessed January 2023.

22 Silvester, NSW Legislative Council debates, 1853, 222–23.

23 A.C.V. Melbourne, *Early Constitutional Development in Australia* (St Lucia: University of Queensland Press, 1963), 400, 404, 426.

24 Silvester, NSW Legislative Council debates, 1853, 39.

25 Silvester, NSW Legislative Council debates, 1853, 47.

26 Silvester, NSW Legislative Council debates, 1853, 47–48.

27 Silvester, NSW Legislative Council debates, 1853, 50.

28 Silvester, NSW Legislative Council debates, 1853, 3.

29 Silvester, NSW Legislative Council debates, 1853, 56.

30 Silvester, NSW Legislative Council debates, 1853, 59.

31 Silvester, NSW Legislative Council debates, 1853, 66–67.

32 Silvester, NSW Legislative Council debates, 1853, 217.

33 Silvester, NSW Legislative Council debates, 1853, 217–18.

34 Silvester, NSW Legislative Council debates, 1853, 86.

35 Silvester, NSW Legislative Council debates, 1853, 87.

36 Silvester, NSW Legislative Council debates, 1853, 87.

37 Silvester, NSW Legislative Council debates, 1853, 88.

38 Silvester, NSW Legislative Council debates, 1853, 134.

39 Silvester, NSW Legislative Council debates, 1853, 146.

40 Silvester, NSW Legislative Council debates, 1853, 166–67.

41 Silvester, NSW Legislative Council debates, 1853, 198.

42 Silvester, NSW Legislative Council debates, 1853, 208.

43 Silvester, NSW Legislative Council debates, 1853, 209.
44 Silvester, NSW Legislative Council debates, 1853, 218.
45 Silvester, NSW Legislative Council debates, 1853, 228.
46 Silvester, NSW Legislative Council debates, 1853, 203–4.
47 Silvester, NSW Legislative Council debates, 1853, 205.
48 Silvester, NSW Legislative Council debates, 1853, 203.
49 Silvester, NSW Legislative Council debates, 1853, 214.
50 Silvester, NSW Legislative Council debates, 1853, 224.
51 Silvester, NSW Legislative Council debates, 1853, 226.
52 CN Connolly, "Politics, Ideology and the New South Wales Legislative Council, 1856–72," PhD thesis, Australian National University, 1974, 19. https://openre-search-repository.anu.edu.au/bitstream/1885/124864/2/b10150663_Connolly_Christopher_Newland.pdf
53 Connolly, "Politics, Ideology and the New South Wales Legislative Council, 1856–72," 1974, 2.
54 Connolly, "Politics, Ideology and the New South Wales Legislative Council, 1856–72," 1974, 19.
55 Connolly, "Politics, Ideology and the New South Wales Legislative Council, 1856–72," 1974, 16.
56 Loveday, Parliamentary factions, 1966, 24.
57 Loveday, Parliamentary factions, 1966, 29.
58 Loveday, Parliamentary factions, 1966, 25.
59 Sydney Morning Herald, 7 May 1858, 2.
60 There is no official NSW Hansard for this period, and newspaper reports are the most authoritative.
61 Sydney Morning Herald, 7 May 1858, 2–3.
62 Sydney Morning Herald, 7 May 1858, 3–4.
63 Sydney Morning Herald, 13 May 1858, 2.
64 Sydney Morning Herald, 13 May 1858, 4.
65 CN Connolly, "Politics, Ideology and the New South Wales Legislative Council, 1856–72," PhD thesis, Australian National University, 1974, 128–29. b10150663_Connolly_Christopher_Newland (2).pdf, accessed February 2023.
66 Sydney Morning Herald, 9 September 1858.
67 CN Connolly, "Politics, Ideology and the New South Wales Legislative Council, 1856–72," PhD thesis, Australian National University, 1974, 128–29. b10150663_Connolly_Christopher_Newland (2).pdf, accessed February 2023.
68 B Nairn, "Robertson, Sir John (1816–1891)," Australian Dictionary of Biography, Volume 6, 1976. Biography – Sir John Robertson – Australian Dictionary of Biography (anu.edu.au), accessed February 2023.

Bibliography

Books and PhD thesis

Cochrane, Peter. *Colonial Ambition*. Carlton: Melbourne University Press, 2006.
Commonwealth Bureau of Census and Statistics, Melbourne, Official Year Book of the Commonwealth of Australia, Containing Authoritative Statistics for the Period 1901-1907, and corrected Statistics for the Period 1788 to 1900. No.1 – 1908. Published: Under the Authority of the Minister of Home Affairs, by G.H.Knibbs, Fellow of the Royal Statistical Society, etc. etc., Commonwealth Statistician. By Authority. Mc-Carron, Bird and Co., Printers, Collins Street, Melbourne.

Connolly, Christopher. N. *"Politics, Ideology and the New South Wales Legislative Council, 1856–72."* PhD thesis, Australian National University, 1974, 30. https://openresearch-repository.anu.edu.au/bitstream/1885/124864/2/b10150663_Connolly_Christopher_Newland.pdf

Curthoys, Ann, and Mitchell Jessie. *Taking Liberty.* Cambridge: Cambridge University Press, 2018.

Dilke, Charles. *Greater Britain.* London: Macmillan and Co., 1907.

Gamboz, Chiara. *"Petitions from Indigenous Australians: Emergence and Negotiations of Indigenous Authorship and Writings."* Unpublished PhD thesis, 2012, 42. Downloaded from http://hdl.handle.net/1959.4/52311 in https://unsworks.unsw.edu.au

Hamilton, Reg. *Colony: Strange Origins of One of the Earliest Modern Democracies.* Kent Town, South Australia: Wakefield Press. 2010.

Hasluck, Alexandra, ed. *Audrey Tennyson's Vice-Regal Days.* Canberra: National Library of Australia, 1978.

Irving, Terence. The Southern Tree of Liberty Explained: class struggle, popular democracy and representative government in New South Wales, *Marxist Left Review* 9 (2015): 119–136.

Irving, Terry. *Southern Tree of Liberty*, Annandale, N.S.W.: Federation Press, (2006): 189.

Keane, John. *The Life and Death of Democracy.* London, Simon & Schuster UK Ltd, (2009): 520.

Loveday, P., and A. W. Martin. *Parliament Factions and Parties, the First Thirty Years of Responsible Government in New South Wales.* Carlton, Victoria, Melbourne University Press, 1966.

McLean, Ian. W. *Why Australia Prospered: The Shifting Sources of Economic Growth.* Princeton, New Jersey, Princeton University Press, 2013.

McMinn, Winston. G. *A Constitutional History of Australia.* Melbourne: Oxford University Press 1979.

Melbourne, Alexander. C. V. *Early Constitutional Development in Australia.* St Lucia, University of Queensland Press, 1963.

Silvester, Edward K, ed. *New South Wales Constitution Bill: The Speeches, in the Legislative Council of New South Wales, on the Second Reading of the Bill for Framing a New Constitution for the Colony*, Thomas Daniel, York Street, Sydney 1853.

Sweetman, Edward. *Australian Constitutional Development.* Melbourne, Macmillan & Co Limited in association with Melbourne University Press, 1925.

Articles and chapters

Curthoys, Ann, and Mitchell Jessie. "The Advent of Self-Government." In *The Cambridge History of Australia*, edited by Alison Bashford and Stuart Macintyre, vol. 1. Port Melbourne, Vic.: Cambridge University Press, 2013.

Nairn, B. "Robertson, Sir John (1816–1891)." *Australian Dictionary of Biography*, vol. 6. Melbourne: Melbourne University Press, 1976.

Phillips, John A., and Charles Wetherell. "The Great Reform Act of 1832 and the Political Modernisation of England." *The American Historical Review* 100 (Apr. 1993).

Scalmer, Sean. "Containing Contention: a Reinterpretation of Democratic Change and Electoral Reform in the Australian colonies." *Australian Historical Studies* 42, no. 3, (September 2011).

Legal

Victorian Constitution 1855
NSW Constitution 1855
South Australian Constitution 1856.
The Electoral Legislation Amendment (Electoral Equality) Act 2021
Wylde v Attorney General of NSW (1948) 78 –CLR 224.
The New South Wales Act 1823 (UK)
NSW Constitution Act 1842 (UK)

Newspapers and other

Sydney Morning Herald.

7   Victoria

The colony of the goldfields and Eureka stockade

Abstract

The Victorian Legislative Council elected in 1851 was a 'mockery of representation' and drafted a constitution which provided for property qualifications for both a Legislative Assembly and Legislative Council, including property qualifications for standing for election. This restricted radicals but others as well. Premier William Clark Haines removed the property qualifications for the Legislative Assembly in 1857 but retained unequal electoral districts. Property qualifications remained for elections to the Legislative Council, which led to periodic political crises as the Council rejected and amended legislation, such as payment of members and land reform, passed by the more democratic Legislative Assembly.

Victoria becomes a colony and the Legislative Council drafts a conservative self-governing constitution

Victoria became a colony separate from NSW on 1 July 1851. Writs for the first election to the new two thirds elected, one third nominated Victorian Legislative Council were issued on the same day, and the new Council first sat on 11 November 1851. The elections were held under the Australia Constitution Act 1850 property qualification requirement.[1]

The electorates were unequal and heavily weighted to the country: the electorates of Evelyn and Mornington, with a combined population of only 879, received a representative, while Melbourne, with 23,143 had only 3 members.[2]

The Argus called the new Council unrepresentative, 'simply a mockery of representation,' and marked all its reports on Council proceedings in 1852 with that damning qualification.[3] As in New South Wales its connection with popular opinion was tenuous, except on issues such as the need for self-government.

The Eureka stockade rebellion on the goldfields influenced the democracy debates in Victoria. In 1853 angry miners rebelled, objecting to expensive mining licences. This ended in a shoot-out with troopers (paid for by Victorian taxes) in which at least 22 miners and five troopers were killed.

DOI: 10.4324/9781003490739-8

There was also a Chartist petition already discussed. The goldfields were central to the later democracy debate, with for example Premier Haines accused by the Leader of the Opposition O'Shanassy of including residency requirements for voting rights to exclude more iterant miners, as well as the background of radicalism and pressure for democracy. Some Eureka rebels participated in debates on democracy as members of parliament, including J.B. Humffray and Peter Lalor, both elected members for Ballarat in 1855.

1953 Debates on a new constitution

On 1 September 1853, a Select Committee was appointed by the Council to consider and report upon the best form of the Constitution for the Colony. On 9 December 1853 the committee recommended:

a That the Legislature of the Colony should consist of the Governor and of two Houses, to be called the Parliament of Victoria;
b That the two Houses should be designated respectively, 'The Legislative Council' and 'The House of Assembly';
c That the Legislative Council should be elective and should represent the education, wealth, and, more especially, the settled interests of the country.
d That to such a body should be entrusted the Legislative functions of the House of Lords;
e That upon the House of Assembly should be conferred all the rights and powers of the House of Commons;
f That the duration of the House of Assembly should be for three years;
g That the responsible officers should be the Colonial Secretary, to be called in future the Chief Secretary, the Attorney-General, the Colonial Treasurer, to be called in future the Treasurer, the Collector of Customs, to be called in future the Commissioner of Trade and Customs, the Surveyor-General, to be called in future the Commissioner of Crown Lands or Survey, the Postmaster-General, the Solicitor-General, and the Commissioner of Public Works;
h That of the responsible officers of Government, two at least should have seats in the Legislative Council, and two at least have seats in the House of Assembly;
i That all the patronage of the Government should be vested in the Governor;
j That the sum of £50,000 should be reserved on the schedule for public worship, for the advancement of religion, and the promotion of good morals in the Colony of Victoria.[4]

The report did not adopt the term of the British Parliament of up to seven years, the Canadian four, or the Chartist annual elections. In Victoria the terms of Parliament would not exceed five years in duration, later reduced to three.

The first reading of the Bill was held on 15 December and the second reading on 25 January. There was considerable debate in public and in the Legislative Council over the religious grant of £50,000. On 21 March an attempt to remove the grant for public worship was lost by a large majority. The Bill passed its third reading on 24 March 1854.[5]

During the constitutional debates the Legislative Council was dominated by the Colonial Secretary, JLFV ('alphabet') Foster, his cousin Stawell, and the other nominees, who opposed democratic measures but eventually not self-government. The unrepresentative nature of the Council was made even more obvious by the Eureka stockade insurrection. Meetings on the goldfields blamed the Colonial Secretary, JLVF Foster for the continuance of the licensing system of the goldfields and demanded his dismissal. Foster, the main architect of the 1855 constitution was forced to resign on 9 December 1854.[6]

JLFV Foster was aware that 'a nominated Upper House is a much more democratic one than an elective one,' mainly because the ministry of the day could swamp a dissident Council.[7]

He therefore carefully designed a constitution which enabled the upper house to 'block any measure it disliked' because of a high property qualification for voting and membership. This it proceeded to do for the rest of the century, causing serious political crises which were only ever partly resolved. Foster stands as the most effective opponent of democracy in the Australian colonies, leaving as his legacy the most powerful, lasting, and obstructive Legislative Council.[8]

'Alphabet' Foster also argued for a theory of responsible government that required a majority in both houses, not just the more democratic Legislative Assembly.[9] He sought an equivalent of the British interest group Constitution:

> The main features of the Constitution under which we exist at home no doubt are the regal, the aristocratical, and democratical, or rather instead of the last terms I would use those of the nobility and the commons; for by a commonalty or a democracy I mean the same. Democracy means the power of the people, and by the people I mean in general the commons, – not one class of the people alone but all classes of the people combined. By the commons the great public power and the great success which have attended our Nation have been attained.[10]

This was the model he wished to follow:

> I do not think we can err in taking as a model our mother country, the Constitution of which has excited the admiration of the whole world, and has been imitated by many who have failed, and by whose errors we may profit; and I must say, Sir, that I should be very doubtful of our success if I did not feel that we are a people who have been brought up under that

Constitution. I know, Sir, that some people may suggest that those who only imitate betray no originality of thought, and that they seem afraid of exercising their own powers in creating a Constitution. I confess I am not one of those ....[11]

He claimed that the terms 'conservatives, liberals and radicals' were not 'applicable here' because the institutions which led to these terms are not present here.[12] He was, however, more obviously an opponent of democratisation, given the design of the constitution. He said:

> Sir, I do believe that the Upper House, elected as we propose, will possess that power and that steadiness, and I am not very far from thinking that perhaps in after years it would be found, as in America, that the Upper House will possess practically more power than the lower. I think it will always be enabled not perhaps to stop the proceedings of the Lower House and year after year bar their progress, but will be strong enough to check their progress until such calm discussion has caused as will really test the merits of any measure, and until an appeal can be made to the colonists at large to know whether the Lower House, as then elected does really express the feelings and opinions of the colonists. Sir, I have heard it stated out of doors that one of the objections to the Upper House which we now propose is that it will be so strong as to lead legislation, that, in fact, it will be impossible, if it clashes which the Lower House, for that House to get on at all. I do not think, Sir that its strength would be so omnipotent, but it is not an argument that weighs much with me against it.[13]

Foster said that the British Constitution divided the legislature into three parts, the Queen, the Lords, and the Commons. He used Blackstone to conclude that the commons are deliberately limited in the right of representation to avoid the lower classes with no stake in the country:

> Now, Sir, what do we find laid down by Sir William Blackstone, and other jurists, as to the right of representation which it is supposed in theory originally resided in the Commons? Sir, you will find it there laid down, that it is supposed that the right of representation was originally universal, that every free man had a right to vote at an election for Members of Parliament. But why does the same eminent writer lay it down that that right has been limited? It was because when they came to the lower classes of the people, they found there those, who having no stake in the country, and but little information, and not possessing many of the exalted feelings which in other classes are to be found, did not value their votes at all beyond the price which they could get for them; and who, not feeling an interest in the success of the nation were open to great bribery, and therefore, the only practical way of guarding against such evils was, that in very early times indeed,

the right of representation was taken away from those who did not possess a freehold of forty shillings a year, or sundry other tenures of different kinds. We propose to make the right of representation wider than we find it to be in England, extended even as that has been by recent legislation. If anyone takes the trouble of looking at the franchise which we propose to give to electors to the Lower House, I think they will agree with me that nobody can be excluded from it except by his own default ....[14]

He said that the upper house would be 'analagous to the House of Lords,' that 'hereditary nominees here ... is impossible at present,' because of 'public opinion,' and because there is in Victoria no 'class of men who would give weight, and influence, and prestige to such a position,' but that the upper house would as in America be found that the upper house is more powerful than the lower:

> perhaps in after years it will be found, as in America, that the Upper House will possess practically more power than the lower. I think it will always be enabled not perhaps to stop the proceedings of the Lower House and year after year bar their progress, but it will be strong enough to check their progress until calm discussion has caused as will really test the merits of any measure, and until an appeal can be made to the colonists at large to know whether the Lower House, as then elected, does really express the feelings and opinions of the colonists.[15]

Foster's justification for the strict conditions for membership of the Legislative Council was that 'greater steadiness of conduct and of legislation, is to be observed in those who possess, first of all, age.'[16] He therefore proposed a requirement that the member be 30 years of age.

To justify a requirement of property-holding, he said:

> We also having observed that wealth generally gave a man very steady ideas, thought it very desirable that in the Legislative Council we should have none but men who did possess that stake in the country; that in fact, all adventurers should be practically excluded from it. I do not think that those gentlemen whom, without any disrespect, I have termed adventurers, ought to be in the Upper House: they will have ample scope for the display of their talent and ambition in the Lower House.[17]

He considered a system of 'double election, either by means of Electoral Colleges or municipal authorities' but 'municipal authorities do not exist here,' although this would be 'the most perfect plan of all.'[18]

He also supported a requirement of reading and writing skills to exercise the franchise.[19]

He supported the 'Royal veto' of legislation and 'the responsibility of the Government to the Legislature' by providing that at least four members of the Government should have a seat in one of the two houses.[20]

He concluded by stating that Victorians were colonists of the Australian branch of the British Empire, and some provision for a confederation of the Australian colonies should be made:

> We wish to be part and parcel of the British empire, we wish to introduce into this colony the main principles upon which the Constitution of Great Britain is founded, and to enjoy here all the liberties and the privileges which our fellow countrymen do at home, and I do trust that under the proposed Bill we shall substantially enjoy them. … We are colonists of the Australian branch of the British Empire, and as there are many subject of mutual interest to the different Australian colonies, in my opinion some provision ought to be made for their confederation.[21]

Mr. O'Shanassy said that:

> there are many points in the Bill which I shall offer very great opposition and objection to, but in the framework of the proposed Constitution for this country I shall offer no objection whatever. That it is desirable there should be three independent and co-existent powers to govern people of British origin with wisdom and justice, is, I believe, as certain as any truth to be laid down in political science, and therefore I think there can be no doubt that it is necessary for us to establish and create three powers.[22]

He said that the Australia Constitutions Act 1850 was 'rendered thoroughly defective by the squatting power in the Legislature of New South Wales.'[23]

He supported an upper house based on a property qualification, but less than proposed by Foster, citing English history, saying that 'property, intelligence and population should be fairly represented.'[24]

Mr. Griffiths reviewed the American constitution, de Tocqueville, and Lord Brougham, and said that the House of Lords could be 'swamped,' Lord Grey intended to do this to pass the Reform Bill but did not have to. He said that the power of the proposed upper house 'of absolutely stopping the whole legislation of the country, and opposing the wishes of the whole people; that is to thirteen men you delegate this power … there is no power short of a Revolution that can affect it. I certainly think that is a very grave objection.'[25]

Mr. Fawkner said that the requirement of a two-thirds majority in each house to change the constitution was inconsistent with the British Constitution which was 'constantly changing.'[26]

Dr. Greeves quoted Lord Grey and Mr. Gladstone, the Bishop of Oxford on upper houses, and Lord Russell concluding that a two-thirds majority requirement for change was necessary 'to prevent any sudden and unnecessary change being introduced.'[27]

The Attorney-General said 'I cannot admit, Sir, either, that we are legislating under the slightest restrictions.' He said that 'the colony is essentially unsuited to a House of Lords; the very fact of emigrating has a tendency to render us all equal ....' He said that 'the time may probably come when it may be to the advantage of the mother country, and of the colony, that both should be separate... I trust not in the lives of any one of us here now ....'[28]

Mr. O'Brien said that he supported five year not three-year terms.[29]

Mr. Goodman said that 'the only safeguard I can see for having Conservatism in the two Houses is to make the qualification a property one ... for men who are men of property will respect the rights of property, and respect good order, and good government.' He said, 'Let us hope that the land shall be fully open to everyone as it is at present really' and the squatters gone.[30]

Mr. Myles noted that there had been little public discussion on the Constitution and questioned why a 12-month residentiary requirement was needed.

Mr. Charlton said public apathy about the Constitution was because 'people are anxious to have the control of their lands' and not delay the Constitution. He said the land requirements to be eligible for election to the upper house would exclude 'many merchants who have a large stake in the interests of the colony.'[31]

The Surveyor-General said that two colonies were seeking a nominee upper house not an elected one and that England tried but failed to make an acceptable constitution for us had given us the power to make on ourselves. He said that we 'have no precedents, no traditions, no former practice to lead us.'[32]

Dr. Murphy quoted Foster on the qualities needed for the upper house, men whom colonists 'look up with respect, men of virtue in the community who ... are regarded with admiration, and whose private and public worth we may at all times be proud.' He questioned whether the possession of £10,000 'does ensure the accompaniment of any of these virtues?' He asked what would happen if the upper house was composed of 13 squatters with a majority ruling over crown lands.[33]

The Collector of Customs said that there were many colonies but 'the present is almost the only case in which a Colony has been, almost without restriction, called upon to propound for itself ... its wishes and its views.' He said that responsible government is 'an experiment' He said that Pitt, Fox and Burke, and Sheridan got into the House of Commons by nomination. This does not mean 'we decry the elective principle, and render it a mockery here.'[34]

Mr. Haines said 'I am in favour of an elective Upper House. I see very great objections to the system of mediate election' and that 'in America the tyranny of the majority is one of the greatest evils that that country suffers under.' He supported a high property qualification because it is better to start too high than too low, because it could be lowered but could not be raised if it was too low.[35]

Mr. Foster noted that only one member supported a nominee upper house.[36]

The resulting constitution was complicated and highly technical in its attempts to restrict and provide for democracy.

It provided for elected upper and lower houses, both with a seat weighting that favoured the more conservative country over the more radical Melbourne. With about one-third of the colony's population, Melbourne was given only one-sixth of the seats. Only men aged 30 or over could sit as a member of the Legislative Council. Members of the Council held office for ten years and were elected six at a time every two years. This was accepted by the Colonial Office.[37]

To stand for the Legislative Assembly required ownership of land worth £2,000 or rental £200. To vote for the Assembly required ownership of land of £50 or an annual rental value of £5.[38] To stand for the Legislative Council required ownership of land worth £5,000 or an annual value of £500.[39] To vote required ownership of land worth £1,000 or annual rental of £100.[40]

Both the NSW and Victorian constitutions received the royal assent on 16 July 1855 and came into force in November. These colonies now had responsible a government, with a largely, though not fully, democratic lower house and an upper house established on a different basis, which would act as a check on 'hasty legislation' made by the more democratic lower house.[41] They had five-year terms.[42]

The Secret Ballot 1856

The Legislative Council passed the Electoral Act 1856 on 13 March 1856 by one vote,[43] which introduced the secret ballot, the first Australian colony to do so.

Premier Haines' government was reluctant and opposed. The Attorney-General said it would not be successful, that it is 'so cumbrous and heavy as to be totally inoperative; whilst the amount of expense that would be entailed, he should be sorry to mention. However the House had determined upon trying this experiment, and he only hoped that in adopting it the House had not put a stop to all elections.' Mr. Greeves and Mr. Hodgson agreed, accusing ballot supporters of obtaining approval of the house for the ballot then leaving the work of developing details to the Government.[44] The man who moved that elections be conducted by secret ballot, William Nicholson, said it would prevent voter intimidation and stop 'the practice of treating and so make elections more orderly' because no-one would buy someone a drink if they couldn't check on how they voted. Nicholson however could not himself develop a workable system of implementing it. Haines resigned on losing the vote but was soon back in power. It was left to Henry Chapman, another member of the Legislative Council, to draft practical means of implementing the ballot, namely the voter arrives at the voting station and is given a voting paper and retires to one of several private booths to vote in secrecy, and then places the folded paper in the ballot box. This worked and was followed throughout the world.[45]

Figure 7.1 William Clark Haines, Premier of Victoria, gave all men the vote in 1857

Elections were held 23 September–24 October 1856 using the secret ballot. The first parliament under the new constitution met in November 1856.

The elections of 1856

The elections of 23 September–24 October 1856 were under a system of unequal electorates, with votes per seat ranging from 3,693 in the Ovens district to 127 in the Colac district. The 13 squatting seats averaged 250 voters while the 18 for Melbourne and Geelong 1,350. The resulting Legislative Assembly was composed of 16 professionals, 18 landed and pastoral, 23 trading, 1 manufacturing, and 1 digger (Lalor, an appointed government official).[46] This led to fewer candidates. In addition, Victoria, unlike South Australia and NSW, had a property qualification for standing. The conservative Stawell had to buy land for the first time and others such as the goldfields radical Humffray entered dubious private arrangements. Only about one-sixth of adult males voted, only about 40 per cent were on the electoral roll.[47]

The 1856 election itself was influenced by 'numerous nebulous reforms associations ... Chartist in outline.' They supported 'abolition of the property qualification for members and the establishment of universal manhood suffrage. At the same time there was a great cry for redistribution of seats and in the first parliament these three demands were answered.'[48]

William Clark Haines, a member of the Legislative Assembly, former surgeon and inarticulate, led the first ministry under self-government.[49] His government was unstable in a parliament of independents without organised political parties and faced with a relatively united opposition under the leadership of John O'Shanassy. It was the first self-government in Victoria. One count was that there were 20 government supporters, 20 'extreme Opposition,' and the rest waverers or likely opposition. The goldfields and Catholics were largely opposition, while the squatters and Anglicans were with the government, and 'merchants often in the middle.'[50]

One man, one vote 1857 and unequal electoral districts justified

In December 1856 Premier William Clark Haines introduced the Electoral Act Amendment Bill, which introduced one man, one vote. In contrast to the secret ballot, this was a Government measure. Under the Bill all men aged 21 or over were given the vote, with residential and citizenship requirements,[51] excluding only those with no stake or footing in the colony.[52]

Figure 7.2 John O'Shanassy, leader of the opposition

During the 1856 debate it was acknowledged that it was no longer the case that men of property were the Victorian electorate. The holders of mining licences were entitled to vote under the original formulation, and the price of a miner's licence had dropped to only £1. This was something approaching one man, one vote. The 1856 amendments were an attempt to 'simplify the existing law,' according to Mr. Fellows.[53]

However, Premier Haines also supported plural voting, a right to vote in any electorate where an elector had property, unequal electorates, and residential qualifications for voting. These were successfully defended by Haines and opposed by O'Shanassy.[54] The Legislative Council elected on a large property qualification remained.

The secret ballot had been introduced early in 1856 and used in the 1856 election, a practical and workable system that was copied, although others such as France, Belgium, Switzerland, and many US States already had secret voting.[55]

Debate on the Electoral Act Amendment Bill was wide-ranging. O'Shanassy implicitly invoked John Locke, saying that working men were men of property because they owned their own labour.[56] The examples of other liberal democracies of the time, the United Kingdom and the United States, were discussed in contrast to the autocracies of Europe and elsewhere. Haines was concerned about the potential for a clash between a Legislative Assembly based on one man, one vote and a Legislative Council with a property requirement for voting,[57] a clash which was indeed a serious problem well into the 20th century. Mr Michie said he supported votes for women and said he knew many who were 'much better fitted for exercise of the franchise than members of the male sex'.[58]

The most wide-ranging discussion of the right to vote as the foundation of modern liberties was given by an opposition member, Mr Fyfe. He referred to the 'sovereignty of the people,' declaring that man had a right to political privileges, which was 'the law of nature which is anterior to all written law'; he believed in moral right, 'which is or ought to be the foundation of all social or political law; and by the express provision of the great charter of English liberty, everything that a man possessed was absolutely his own, and to take away anything from him without his consent, is a violation of this great original law of nature, and of the rights of man; and it was for the protection of this great natural and moral right that the elective franchise was conferred, and a representative form of government created. If a man were deprived of those rights and yet compelled to pay towards the public revenue, an injustice was perpetrated on him. Strictly speaking, a property qualification gave a man no right at all. It gave him influence, and would perhaps influence elections, as the man who spent the most money on an election would in all probably gain it.'[59]

These were amendments directed at the special circumstances of the colony of Victoria. This included the large and turbulent goldfields, which had just seen the armed conflict of the Eureka Stockade in Ballarat, an uprising over miners' licences during which miners were killed by soldiers and soldiers by miners.

The opposition was concerned that new provisions for registration to vote might be difficult for miners to comply with and contended that they were being excluded from voting. Mr. Michie asked if the

> Hon. Gentlemen opposite suppose that the gentlemen with yellow clay on their trousers, coming up from their holes or deep sinkings, would fill up a claim in the form prescribed by the schedule to the Act, and forward it within the required time to the 'clerk of the Parliament'? … would they not be practically disenfranchised?[60]

Mr. Pyke said that the requirement of 'continued residence – to a class continually moving from place to place, were a mockery and virtually disenfranchised them.'[61]

Mr. Fellows said that the registration system involved 'educational tests' which he opposed, given that at least once dignitary in the church in Melbourne had 'handwriting ordinary men would have very great difficulty in deciphering.'[62]

Mr. O'Shanassy said that the bill's registration provisions were 'an attempt to preserve the ultra conservative view in a democratic body' because miners had trouble meeting residence requirements.[63] O'Shanassy and his supporters voted against the bill (which nevertheless passed).

Mr. Evans said he 'proposed to confer the power of voting on all persons who were admitted to the benefits of naturalisation. If it be proper to revise the naturalisation laws, let them do so; and if it was thought to be desirable to exclude the Chinese from the privileges of naturalisation, let them do so; but, he repeated, he went on the principle that when they granted the privilege, of naturalisation which admitted the subjects of them to any other office of trust in the colony -even to that of an inspector of railways-he did not see why they should exclude them from the elective franchise.' [64]

Mr. Haines said 'he should like to inform the hon. Member for Richmond, and the House generally that, at the time when the Constitution Act was considered, it was laid down as a principle that it was desirable for foreigners who came to the colony to remain subject to the laws for some time, that they might understand them before they were entitled to participate in framing them. If, for instance, persons came to this country from a despotic country, the desirability of preventing such persons from mixing in their politics for some time was very obvious. The amendment was then put and negatived.'

Mr. Greeves' amendment was also put and negatived. Mr. Fyfe then moved, as a further amendment that the word 'two' be substituted for the word 'three.' 'Three years, he thought, was too long for Germans and too short for Chinese.'

Mr. Myles suggested that the better course to adopt was to amend the Naturalisation Act. He contended that they ought to open a door as widely as possible to enable such persons who were entitled to hold property and to become members of municipal councils to use the franchise. He intended to move that the word 'three' be struck out and that its place remain blank.

Captain Clarke 'called the attention of the House to the fact that the expunging of the fourth clause was a matter of great importance, as it would involve the establishing of equal electoral districts. That must be the next step. Population, property, and area guided the old House in the formation of the electoral districts, and was that to be now overthrown and the electoral areas based solely on population as a consequence of manhood suffrage.'[65]

Premier Haines welcomed migrants, saying that:

'They were there, at the antipodes of the mother country, proposing to lay the foundation of what he believed would be a great Empire, and it would not be proper for them, he considered, to confine citizenship to those persons who were born in the United Kingdom. He was in favour of opening the doors of the Constitution to the natives of every country under heaven, and especially to the United States, and those countries of Europe who enjoyed the same constitution, professed the same religion, and in many instances spoke the same languages as themselves. In the colony there were at the present time, 10,000 natives of Germany – men of a kindred race and religion, and almost of the same language as themselves [a laugh] … Let the people know on the banks of the Rhine, under the despotic government of Austria, at the foot of the Alps, in Switzerland and in Holland, that so soon as they landed in Australia, they would be entitled to all the privileges of naturalization, and to all the advantages of subjects of the British Crown.

…

No doubt such information would invite the emigration of that useful class of men. Instead, therefore, of the amendment, he would suggest to the hon. member to strike out the clause altogether. So soon as all foreigners were admitted to the privileges of citizenship they should be entitled to the privilege of voting for representatives to that Home.'[66]

Mr. Haines then moved for multiple voting entitlements, a voting right in any electoral district where a voter held property of 50 pounds:

Clause 4th-Every such male person as aforesaid who shall be seised at law, or in equity of lands or tenements for his own life or (or the life of any other person or for any larger estate of the clear value of fifty pounds or of the clear yearly value of five pounds shall be qualified to vote in the election of members of the Legislative Assembly for the electoral district in which such lands or tenements shall be situate.

Mr. O'Shannassy said that clause 4 should be struck out:

The question which they had to consider was whether the policy of the representation of the people in that Assembly should be constructed on the widest possible basis, or on the contrary that persons having property should counteract the influence of manhood suffrage. Every man in this Colony possessed property, and when they conferred the franchise on manhood, they conferred on property its rights (Oh. oh). Was not labor property'? He repeated that they conferred on property its rights when they conferred the franchise on persons of twenty one years of age. Property was fairly provided for by the other branch of the Legislature, and he hoped Hon. members would not lose sight of that fact. This franchise would add considerably to the electoral roll if it were not clogged by the registration clauses. The hon. member for Collingwood had presented a petition on the previous day from certain electors of Collingwood who stated it as their opinion that if the 4th clause were struck out many of them would be deprived of their franchise. (Hear, from Mr. Embling.) He should like to know more distinctly than from the cry of 'hear,' how they came to this conclusion. He was unchanged in opinion with regard to the desirability of conceding universal suffrage to the people. The Assembly he thought, as the House of Commons, ought to represent the popular will and the other branch of the Legislature the property of the colony, and the two qualifications should be kept distinct, so far as the electors were concerned. He would say no more, but content himself with moving that the 4th clause be struck out.

Captain Clarke said it was going 'too far at present' to delete clause 4 and have electoral districts set entirely on population and manhood suffrage and remove property rights.

Dr. Embling said that owners of property should have the right to vote and not be overridden by the city.

Mr. Fellows said 'The only way to keep the balance of representation was to allow property to be represented as well as individuals.'

Mr. Pyke said that 'Manhood suffrage embraced the doctrine of complete political equality, and Hon. members imagined that having conceded this in the third clause, they were at liberty to indulge their anti-progressive tendencies by restricting it in a subsequent one.'

Mr. Owens said multiple voting would 'practically demolish the extension of the franchise to all.'

Mr. Griffith said 'He believed that this clause diluted the principle of manhood suffrage-(hear);- but at the same time he felt that property should be represented in that House as well as labour.'

Mr. Haines said that he did not support 'naked democracy' and supported multiple voting. To do otherwise would threaten the connection with the monarchy and 'mother country.' Did members wish to admit women to the vote or minors committing felony? 'Manhood suffrage is not universal suffrage ….'

Mr. Michie said that clause 4 would lead as James Mill, father of John Stuart Mill, had shown to the domination of the popular element by the aristocracy.

Mr. Campbell said 'The fourth clause represented and conserved an element which had always existed in the mother country and from thence had been introduced into this colony. Under it political interests had grown, and rights and privileges had accrued, which the excision of the fourth clause would remove and altogether destroy.'

Mr. Duffy said 'Both the Hon. gentlemen seemed strangely alarmed at the consequences of the establishment of universal suffrage in this country; but it arose, he considered, from an old English prejudice. If they applied the principle to a country where great properties existed, and the people there were suddenly enfranchised, then there might be danger from the sudden extreme. But here the progress of the acquirement of property by the people was an everyday thing, and the gradual accumulation prevented even the anticipation of danger.'

…

'The Hon. member was also afraid if we had universal suffrage we should first elect our own Governor, and then the connection with the mother country would rapidly cease. That meant if the people had their way they would throw off their allegiance to the mother-country. (Hear, hear.) In point of fact, however, he did not consider that was the case. There was no eager desire for it on the part of any constituency. (Hear, hear.).'

Mr. Stawell said 'He took it their object ought to be fair representation of every interest and he contended if property was not represented, one class in the community would not be represented, and then class legislation would follow.'

Mr. Blair said that 'If he understood the suffrage at all, it ought to based on simple citizenship and that alone.'

The House divided and clause 4 was retained 29–24.[67] Plural voting was approved.

The new Victorian constitution gave the vote to all adult men naturalised or deemed naturalised with a residence qualification of 12 months in elections to the Legislative Assembly.[68] The Legislative Council had a property qualification of owning freehold of £100 or holding lands for life worth £1,000, plus graduates and certain professionals in Victoria.[69] Plural voting, voting in more than one electorate, was permissible, and unequal electorates remained.

There was still no mechanism for resolving disputes between the upper and lower houses, 'with disastrous results' of over a century of unresolvable political disputes.[70]

Notes

1 Male owners of freehold worth £100, and the occupiers of dwellings worth a rental of £10 per annum.

2 Edward Sweetman, *Constitutional Development of Victoria, 1851–6* (Melbourne: Whitcombe & Tombs Limited, 1920), 106.

3 John Waugh, "Framing the First Victorian Constitution, 1853–5 [1997]," *Monash University Law Review* 21; 23, no. 2 (1997): 331, 332.

4 Edward Sweetman, *Constitutional Development of Victoria, 1851–6* (Melbourne: Whitcombe & Tombs Limited, 1920), 45–48.

5 Sweetman, *Constitutional Development of Victoria, 1851–6*, (Melbourne: Whitcombe & Tombs Limited) 1920, 45–48.

6 Sweetman, *Constitutional Development of Victoria, 1851–6*, (Melbourne: Whitcombe & Tombs Limited) 1920, 50.

7 G. Serle, "The Victorian Legislative Council, 1856–1950," in *Historical Studies: Selected Articles,* first series, ed. J.J. Eastwood and F.B. Smith (Carlton: Melbourne University Press, 1964), 128ff.

8 F. Bongiorno, *Dreamers and schemers* (Melbourne: La Trobe University Press, 2022), 44–45.

9 Webb, Victorian Legislative Council debates, 1854, 16.

10 Webb, Victorian Legislative Council debates, 1854, 3

11 Webb, Victorian Legislative Council debates, 1854, 4.

12 Webb, Victorian Legislative Council debates, 1854, 4.

13 Webb, Victorian Legislative Council debates, 1854, 10.

14 Webb, Victorian Legislative Council debates, 1854, 5.

15 Webb, Victorian Legislative Council debates, 1854, 9–10

16 Webb, Victorian Legislative Council debates, 1854, 10.

17 Webb, Victorian Legislative Council debates, 1854, 14.

18 Webb, Victorian Legislative Council debates, 1854, 12.

19 Webb, Victorian Legislative Council debates, 1854, 7.

20 Webb, Victorian Legislative Council debates, 1854, 15–16.

21 Webb, Victorian Legislative Council debates, 1854, 17.

22 Webb, Victorian Legislative Council debates, 1854, 20.

23 Webb, Victorian Legislative Council debates, 1854, 22.

24 Webb, Victorian Legislative Council debates, 1854, 25–26.

25 Webb, Victorian Legislative Council debates, 1854, 40.

26 Webb, Victorian Legislative Council debates, 1854, 42.

27 Webb, Victorian Legislative Council debates, 1854, 56.

28 Webb, Victorian Legislative Council debates, 1854, 67–77.

29 Webb, Victorian Legislative Council debates, 1854, 78.

30 Webb, Victorian Legislative Council debates, 1854, 81–82.

31 Webb, Victorian Legislative Council debates, 1854, 85–87.

32 Webb, Victorian Legislative Council debates, 1854, 91–93.

33 Webb, Victorian Legislative Council debates, 1854, 103–6.

34 Webb, Victorian Legislative Council debates, 1854, 120–33.

35 Webb, Victorian Legislative Council debates, 1854, 139.

36 Webb, Victorian Legislative Council debates, 1854, 141.

37 W.G. McMinn, *A Constitutional History of Australia* (Melbourne: Oxford University Press, 1979), 54.

38 Victorian Constitution 1855, clause XI.

39 Victorian Constitution 1855, clause IV.

40 Victorian Constitution 1855, clause V.

41 Victorian Constitution 1855, W.G. McMinn, *A constitutional history of Australia* (Melbourne: Oxford University Press, 1979), 55.

42 Victorian Constitution, clause XIX.
43 Assent given 19 March 1856.
44 The Argus, 13 March 1856.
45 Judith Brett, *From Secret Ballot to Democracy Sausage: How Australia Got Compulsory Voting* (Melbourne: Text Publishing, 2023), 19–23.
46 Joy E. Mills, "The Composition of the Victorian parliament, 1856–1881," *Historical Studies: Australia and New Zealand* 2, no. 5 (1942): 25–39, 31, DOI: 10.1080/10314614208594810
47 Geoffrey Serle, *The Golden Age* (Melbourne: Melbourne University Press, 1977), 256, 264.
48 Joy E. Mills, "The composition of the Victorian parliament, 1856–1881," *Historical Studies: Australia and New Zealand* 2, no. 5 (1942): 25–39, at 27–33, DOI: 10.1080/10314614208594810
49 B. Malone, "Haines, William Clark (1810–1866)," *Australian Dictionary of Biography* 4 (1972). Biography – William Clark Haines – Australian Dictionary of Biography (anu.edu.au).
50 Geoffrey Serle, *The Golden Age* (Melbourne: Melbourne University Press, 1977), 258–59.
51 With a requirement that he be a naturalised citizen or a 'denizen' of two years residence (Hansard, 166, 18 December 1856), or a natural born subject (Hansard, 175, 18 December 1856).
52 Hansard, 10 December 1856, 98.
53 Hansard, 10 December 1856, 100.
54 Geoffrey Serle, *The Golden Age* (Melbourne: Melbourne University Press, 1977), 265.
55 Serle, *The Golden Age*, 1977, 257.
56 Hansard, 18 December 1856, 167.
57 Hansard, 18 December 1856, 170.
58 Hansard, 18 December 1856, 171.
59 Hansard, 10 December 1856, 105.
60 Hansard, 10 December 1856, 102–3.
61 Hansard, 10 December 1856, 103.
62 Hansard, 10 December 1856, 100.
63 Hansard, 10 December 1856, 99.
64 The Chinese Immigration Act 1855 (Vic) restricted immigration of Chinese, which was circumvented by them landing in South Australia and walking to the goldfields.
65 The Chinese Immigration Act 1855 (Vic) restricted the immigration of Chinese, which was circumvented by their landing in South Australia and walking to the goldfields.
66 Hansard, 18 December 1856, 165–66.
67 Hansard, 18 December 1856, 167–73
68 Electoral Act 1857 (Vic), clauses II and III.
69 Electoral Act 1857 (Vic) clauses IV–VII.
70 John Waugh, "Framing the First Victorian Constitution, 1853–5 [1997]," *Monash University Law Review* 21; 23, no. 2 (1997): 331, 360.

Bibliography

Books

Bongiorno, Frank. *Dreamers and Schemers*. Melbourne: La Trobe University Press, 2022.
Brett, Judith, *From Secret Ballot to Democracy Sausage: How Australia Got Compulsory Voting*. Melbourne, Victoria: The Text Publishing Company, 2023.

Malone, B. "Haines, William Clark (1810–1866)," *Australian Dictionary of Biography* vol. 4, Melbourne: Melbourne University Press, 1972.

McMinn, Winston. G., *A Constitutional History of Australia*. Melbourne: Oxford University Press, 1979.

Articles and chapters

Mills, Joy E. "The Composition of the Victorian Parliament, 1856–1881," *Historical Studies: Australia and New Zealand* 2, no. 5 (1942): 25–39, 31. DOI: 10.1080/10314614208594810

Serle, Geoffrey. "The Victorian Legislative Council, 1856–1950," In *Historical Studies: Selected Articles, First Series*, edited by Jennifer. J. Eastwood and F.B. Smith. Carlton: Melbourne University Press, 1964.

Sweetman, Edward, *Constitutional Development of Victoria, 1851–6*. Melbourne: Whitcombe & Tombs Limited, 1920.

Waugh, John. "Framing the First Victorian Constitution, 1853–5 [1997]," *Monash University Law Review* 21; 23, no. 2 (1997): 331.

Webb, George. H. F. *Debate in the Legislative Council of the Colony of Victoria on the Second Reading of the New Constitution Bill*, Melbourne: Caleb Turner, 1854.

Other

The Argus, Melbourne : Argus Office, 1848–1957.13 March 1856

Victorian Hansard, Melbourne: W. Fairfax 1858–1865

Electoral Act 1857 (Vic).

Victorian Constitution 1855 (UK).

8 South Australia

The democracy colony

Abstract

On 21 July 1853 Lieutenant-Governor Young tabled in the Legislative Council a draft constitution providing for a Council nominated for life and property qualifications for voting for the Legislative Assembly. The Colonial Office rejected the constitution. After elections in August 1855, a new Legislative Council developed a compromise Bill of an elected Legislative Council elected by holders of freehold worth £50; leaseholders holding £20 annual value; and tenants of £25 annual rental. The Legislative Assembly would be elected by males over 21. This was a radical constitution; the results of the popular will of electors and opposed by the Governors but not, apparently, the Colonial Office.

A democratic colony

South Australia had bitter ideological arguments about State aid to religion, which differentiated the colony leaders from the established constitution of Britain, with an established church. This distanced South Australia from a common electioneering speech of Tory candidates in Britain: for the Queen, our glorious constitution, and the alters of our established church![1]

South Australia always had democratic inclinations, whether because it was composed only of 'free' settlers and no convicts or the large influence of radical Protestant dissenters who dissented from the established constitution in Britain at least where the established church was concerned[2] or perhaps the endless kangaroo grass. The first democratic election on the Australian continent was to the Adelaide Municipal Council in 1840 (voting limited to men with property of £20 per annum with a six months residency requirement or to stand of £50 or possessed of personal property of £500[3]), and it may have been the world's first use of proportional representation.[4]

While Victoria and Queensland were part of New South Wales and were therefore bound by the Constitution Act 1842 (UK), South Australia was not. It had separate legislation, the South Australian Act 1842 (UK) which repealed the chaotic earlier arrangements of shared power between the Governor and the Colonization Commissioners established with the South Australia

DOI: 10.4324/9781003490739-9

Act 1834 (UK). The shared power led to unworkable competition between the Governor and ambitious individuals such as Commissioner James Hurtle Fisher, the worst sort of quibbling attorney.[5] The 1842 Act replaced this with the more usual arrangement of a Governor and a Legislative Council of at least seven members nominated by the Crown.

Figure 8.1 George Strickland Kingston c1870, radical leader

South Australia even exported its convicted criminals as convicts to the other colonies. It was a 'Province' as well as a colony. Proper young women wore white gloves to public events as late as the 1960s.

The elections of 1851 and 1855

In South Australia 15 out of 16 members elected to the Legislative Council in 1855 (9 were nominated by the Crown) supported the secret ballot, and a majority supported votes for all men.[6] In the 1851 election 13 of the

16 elected members opposed State aid to religion.[7] Unlike the NSW and Victorian Legislative Councils, the South Australian largely represented popular opinion.

The more radical South Australian voting results are not easily explained, given that electorates were weighted towards the country as they were in NSW and Victoria. However, even country electorates such as Noarlunga voted for democrats such as the Protestant dissenter William Peacock in the 1851 election, not Captain O'Halloran, who opposed extreme democratisation. The two candidates toured the local public houses such as the Emu Hotel, the Flag-Staff Hotel, the Farriers Arms, the Bush Inn, the Horseshoe, and St Leonard's Inn, giving rousing speeches.[8] So rousing were the 1851 speeches and riotous behaviour that the South Australian Electoral Act prohibited personal canvassing after 1851, leading to quieter elections through letters to the newspapers setting out policy positions.[9]

Bishop Short's unsympathetic assessment after the 1851 election was that the majority of those elected:

> have been returned by a party ultra-republican in Religion and Politics, men who emigrated from England with embittered political and religious feelings, and who seek to assimilate this Colony in its habits and notions to the United States.[10]

The first draft constitution

In 1852 the two thirds elected, one third nominated South Australian Legislative Council established a Select Committee to report on the Constitution which recommended 'it would be desirable to established two chambers in the Legislature … the Upper House should be elective.'[11]

On 22 September 1852, Francis Dutton gave notice he would move an amendment to provide for one man one vote, the ballot, and abolish property qualifications.

Dutton also moved that the Council request the Lieutenant-Governor to prepare a bill introducing the above amendments.

There appeared to be some support among the nominees for the radicals. On 20 October 1852, the Colonial Secretary gave notice to move that the franchise be extended as proposed by Dutton but requiring 12 months of residence, not 6. Mr. Kingston moved that there be two chambers, one elected by all the registered electors and one by a property franchise of £20.

However, this was short-lived. On 21 July 1853, Lieutenant-Governor Young made a speech to the Legislative Council announcing that he had directed that two bills be prepared to provide for a parliament of two houses, a Legislative Assembly, and a Legislative Council. They would enable 'responsible Government' including of Crown lands to be introduced. The selection

Figure 8.2 Francis Stacker Dutton, radical leader

of members of the Legislative Council was to be vested in the Crown and they would hold office for life as this was 'most accordant with the principles of the British Constitution.' A 'Bill to establish a Parliament in South Australia' was tabled.

Under this bill, passed by the Legislative Council on 10 August 1853[12] and transmitted to the Colonial Office for approval in December 1853, Clauses 4–5 established a Legislative Council of no fewer than 12 nominees, each of whom would hold office 'for the term of his life.'

Clause 10 established a Legislative Assembly to be composed of 36 members elected by men who held property of £20 sterling, or a householder occupying premises of £5 rental value annually, or a leaseholder of property of £10 sterling annually, with six months occupation and no criminal convictions of a certain nature unless pardoned or the sentence served.

The radicals fought the bill. On 5 August 1853, debate was adjourned on Dutton's motion that 'this Council is of opinion that the Upper House should be elective'.

Dutton spoke to his motion, stating:[13]

> How could the Upper House act harmoniously with the Lower Chamber unless the people had a voice in its formation? He was quite satisfied as to the fitness of the people and was prepared to place the trust in their hands.

Mr. Gwynne said his fear was the fear of the tyranny of the democratic majority. Many who thought with him objected to the measure on account of its democratic tendencies. He would be willing to support the measure – to take all risks – if a nominated Upper House were conceded. If they refused a nominee Upper House the Constitution would be nothing more nor less than a pure democracy, and they would soon sink into a republic. He wanted a similar institution to the House of Lords.

Mr. Waterhouse said a second chamber would be a check upon hasty legislation and a link between the Crown and the people. There was no analogy between a nominated Upper House and the House of Lords, nor could we compare this colony and England. People appeared to labour under the apprehension of some indefinable evil connected with an elective Upper House, but such was not a necessary feature of a republic.

Mr. Torrens said an elective Upper House would be but a reflex of the Lower. He did not want to see the Crown's power rendered absolutely null and void. It would be democracy. He who desired to live under the form of constitutional monarchy would vote for an Upper House nominated for life. They were in no position to experimentalise. With the British Constitution they had tried, proved and afforded more true liberty than that of any other country now existing or that ever had existed. In ancient Greece and Rome, the bulk of the people were slaves and helots. In the United States slavery was a national institution. The fruits of an elective Upper House in the United States were popular opinion substituted for law: the judges of the land bowing before it; the rights of property invaded. There reigned the despotism of despotisms – 'the will of the majority!'

Mr. Angas said that in the House of Lords the elective principle to a certain extent obtained. Bishops were elected. The United States had the most perfect system of education and the best modes of religious instruction. If slavery were tolerated this was not the Constitution founded by the descendants of the religious fathers. He did not want to introduce disorder into the colony or separation from the parent State. He possessed large landed property interests and was not indifferent to the issues. He would vote for an elective Upper House.

Mr. Finniss, Colonial Secretary, said that the nominee principle gave large scope for selecting men most distinguished for talent, for information, for wealth. There would be no such scope under the elective principle. The nominee could have no party purpose to serve. If the Governor could abuse power so could the people. An elected Upper House was untried except for the Cape, which was a mere experiment. They would adopt the results of experience rather than untried theories.

Mr. Baker argued in favour of an elective Upper House elected for life. This would be a bulwark against the encroachments of both the Crown and the people, by being elected for life their independence would be secured. If not he would rather accept a nominated Upper House. He wanted a compromise between the Government and the Opposition.

Mr. Kingston said that Mr. Gwynne said an aristocratic form of government was preferable to a democracy, but in the colony, there was no aristocratic class, they were all South Australians. A nominated Upper House would lead to a party spirit because they would never rest until they had got rid of a nominated Upper House.

Mr. Dashwood, Collector of Customs, said he would never vote for a form of Constitution not based upon the model of the British Constitution, or as nearly assimilated to it as circumstances would permit. An elected Upper House would not be independent, while those nominated for life would not be tools of the Governor.

Mr. Bagot said that an Elected Upper House was the best form of Constitution to meet the requirements of the colony, and he was willing to leave the decision to the intelligent people of the colony. A nominated Upper House was an attempt to control and check the popular will, placing the entire control of Government in the hands of a few. A popular measure could be defeated at any time.

Mr. Davenport said that a nominated Upper House was most in accordance with the British Constitution, and the analogy of the British Constitution was the best they could adopt. The House of Lords had displayed more talent, tact, and knowledge in expounding the law than the House of Commons because of an aristocracy of mind. The colony would get on badly unless they had an aristocracy of that kind. An example was the response to Chartism, in which the Government looked on with silent dignity, unlike America in the case of the invasion of Cuba. The Governor had better opportunities of judging the capacities of men, the intellect, talent, and knowledge of the House of Lords was the keystone to the British Constitution.

Mr. Peacock said he would rather lay his head on the block than entail on his children such a farcical imitation of the House of Lords. Nineteen out of 20 colonists would be strenuously opposed to a nominee Upper House.

Mr. Richard Davies Hanson, Advocate-General, said that the House of Lords did not set themselves permanently against the people. Catholic Emancipation, the Reform Bill, and the Repeal of the Corn Laws were carried out against the richest and most potent aristocracy in the world. He wanted independent men in the Upper House who did not look with one eye on merits and another on the desires of their constituents. The opinions of the people were not always correct. He was prepared to yield to the people when he knew that they had time for dispassionate reflection and when a matter was placed before them in all its bearings. The people should submit to the laws.

On 5 August 1853, Mr. Dutton's democracy motion was defeated, 7 ayes to 15 noes.

On 10 August 1853, the Government constitution bill was read a second time, with 17 ayes and 5 noes. It was adjourned into committee debate and passed. On 4 November 1853, a prominent supporter of the bill, Mr Fisher, moved that the Constitution Bill be transmitted to the Secretary of State for the Colonies to proceed with parliamentary enactments to enable this province to avail itself of the provisions of that bill. Mr Kingston moved that the upper house be elective. Kingston's motion was defeated, 5 ayes to 11 noes.

On 6 December 1853, the Lieutenant-Governor informed the Legislative Council that he had transmitted the Constitution Bill to the Secretary of State for the Colonies. On 9 December 1853, the Lieutenant-Governor addressed the Legislative Council and advised that the Constitution Bill had been transmitted.

In September 1853, the Legislative Council passed a resolution opposing a nominated upper house.[14]

In February 1854, the Governor sent to the Colonial Office a memorial signed by five thousand persons, who complained that they had been 'induced to change their wish for an elected Upper Chamber owing solely to' the interpretation they had been given of Colonial Office instructions. They had not been told of Lord Newcastle's revised instructions withdrawing an instruction that the Legislative Council be nominated.

As noted earlier the Secretary of State, Sir John Pakington, sent a memorandum to Governor Fitzroy of NSW on 15 December 1852 in which he advised that 'the Council should establish the new legislature on the basis of an elective Assembly and a Legislative Council to be nominated by the Crown.' He was succeeded in December 1852 by Lord Newcastle who sent a further memorandum on 18 January 1853 indicating more flexibility and who privately supported an elective upper house.[15] Copies were sent to the Lieutenant-Governors of Victoria and South Australia. The Governor failed to notify them of Lord Newcastle's memorandum. The petition protested the proposed life membership of the nominated, unelected upper house, and against property qualifications for lower house electors.

In May 1855 received in South Australia in July 1855, the Colonial Office advised the South Australian Government that it would not proceed in any way with the Constitution.

The second and third draft constitutions

In August 1855 the new governor, Richard MacDonnell Governor set out a proposed Bill to provide for a parliament consisting of a single chamber.[16] He decided to hold another election, for September 1855. He supported a conservative constitution, and distrusted 'pure democracy,' but had support neither from the Council and South Australian colonists nor public support from the Colonial Office.[17]

After the election the new two thirds elected, one third nominated Legislative Council met on 20 November 1855. Mr. Kingston moved that both chambers be elective and:

> The extension of the elective franchise to every male twenty-one years of age, untainted by crime, who has been registered six months in the District ... The qualification for Electors to both Houses to be the same ... No property qualification to be required for Members of either House.

This amendment was withdrawn by leave.

The debate that followed was involved, but the issue of the qualifications for voting was settled relatively quickly. The Constitution Bill committee-stage debate commenced on 10 December 1855. On 18 December the Colonial Secretary moved that the Legislative Council of 18 members be elected by three classes of property holders: holders of freehold worth £50; lease-holders holding £20 annual value; and tenants of £25 annual rental. This was passed with minimal debate.[18]

The Advocate-General moved that:

> Every man of the age of twenty-one years, being a natural-born or naturalised subject of Her Majesty, and having been registered upon the electoral roll of any district for the period of six calendar months prior to any election, shall be qualified to vote in the election of members to serve in the Legislative Assembly.[19]

The motion made exceptions for certain criminal convictions. The Colonial Secretary moved that this be adopted as Clause 15.

Mr. Baker moved that no man could be enrolled who could not read or write. This topic provoked the most debate of any on the issue of voting eligibility. Mr. Bagot said that no man should be deprived of the vote 'whose ignorance was the consequence of poverty or bad government.' Mr. Peacock said that 'there was no fear of ignorant men coming in such swarms as to swamp the colony,' and that such a man 'still might be man of property and sound judgement.'

Mr. Baker accused members of being inconsistent with an earlier debate in 1853 and then suggested that his amendment not come into effect for two years, thus enabling men to gain an education.

Mr. Angas then said he would support this, given that education had been 'established in many districts in the colony, and the facilities for instruction were greatly increased.' Every person could gain an education.

Mr. Reynolds knew 'many men of intelligence, integrity and property who would be disenfranchised by the amendment.' Then, what was meant by the words read and write?

Mr. Kingston said that 'there were many men who arrived in the colony not only without sixpence but unable to read and write; they had by prudence, good conduct intelligence and honesty not only secured property but established an undeniable right to all political privileges which colonists enjoy and it would be unjust to … despoil them of those rights and privileges.'

Mr Dutton said that the clause would 'disenfranchise a large body of meritorious electors.'

Mr Younghusband said that the amendment would 'attach the same penalty to the misfortune of not being able to read and write which the Act imposed on persons convicted of treason and other heinous crimes.'

Mr Scott said that 'no taxation without representation was an established maxim' and the amendment would deprive of representation many who had 'a large stake in the country.' All these speakers opposed the amendment.

The Colonial Secretary supported the amendment because 'it was, at least, a test that the possessor had the tools – the means whereby he might acquire political knowledge.' He suggested that the amendment be remodelled to include those with property. The Advocate-General agreed.

Mr Baker did not do this, given the extent of opposition, but withdrew the amendment and Clause 15 was carried.[20] All men would have the vote even if illiterate.

The Constitution Bill was passed on 2 January 1856. In proroguing the Council Governor Macdonnell said that:

'I confidently expect that the extended political power entrusted to the people of this country, and the universal suffrage conceded by the new Constitution, will prove a safe and conservative measure, and, whilst conferring the utmost possible powers of self-government, will render stronger and more enduring than ever the cherished ties of affection and loyalty which link this Province to the throne of our respected and beloved Sovereign.' He said the session was the longest and most remarkable of the South Australian legislature.

On 11 November 1856, the Lieutenant-Governor read an address in which he advised that the Constitution Bill had been assented to and would be immediately implemented. The new constitution was reserved on 4 January 1856.

The 24 December 1855, the South Australian Register[21] printed and made public a copy of the new constitution providing for a Legislative Assembly of 36 members elected by 'manhood suffrage,' all men voting, and a Legislative Council of 18 members elected by three classes of property holders: holders of freehold worth £50; leaseholders holding £20 annual value; and tenants of £25 annual rental. Parliament had a three-year term.[22]

Given the general ideals constitutions and electoral laws are always 'approaching democracy' but South Australia was remarkably democratic in tendency. The City of Adelaide held the first election in Australia, in October 1840.[23] South Australia provided that evidence from Aboriginal people could be accepted in courts of law without a Christian oath in 1844, the first colony to do so.[24] In 1851 the partly elected Legislative Council ended State aid to religion, the first part of the British Empire to do so.[25] The 1856 Constitution was the most radical in the British Empire, including votes for all men for the Legislative Assembly, the secret ballot, no plural voting, and a lower property qualification for the Legislative Council than Victoria.[26] It gave women the vote in 1895, the second in the world after New Zealand, and gave them the right to stand as members of Parliament, the first in the world.[27]

In addition South Australia was the first part of the British Empire to legalise trade unions in 1876, the first endorsed United Labor Party candidates in Australia were elected in 1891, and in 1896, women voted for the first time in a general election in Australia and the second time in the world.[28]

South Australian campaigns before democracy

South Australia had a history of divisive public campaigns leading up to the democracy debates, including against a proposed mining tax in 1846. A public meeting was held where the pioneer banker Edward Stephens declared that 'Britishers' 'went forth alone and unaided … to add another flourishing Province … English statesmen conveyed the land to us in fee simple.' We discover its riches and they turn round and say, 'we'll trouble you for that back again.' The meeting drew up a petition.

When the Bill came before the Legislative Council on 30 September 1846, the four non-official nominees John Morphett, Captain Bagot, Major O'Halloran, and Samuel Davenport opposed the Bill and when defeated left the Chamber leaving it without a quorum. After anxious communication with the Colonial Secretary Earl Grey, Governor Robe withdrew the Bill. This was widely seen as a conflict between the Governor and the people, and as showing the need for constitutional change.[29]

When the Governor decided to tax drays and carriages in 1850, anti-dray tax associations were formed, and a rowdy public campaign started with the slogan 'no taxation without representation,' after comparisons were made of taxation of British people living in Britain and British people in South Australia. Plans were made to register only a few days between them and interchange licence plates and go to town on different days but were abandoned. There was even a song 'a coward slave is he who pays.'[30]

State aid to religion

However, what made South Australia unusual was State aid to religion, which preoccupied the colonists as much as or even more than self-government and democracy and led to bitter electoral campaigns and considerable debate in the Legislative Council.

On 24 June 1846 Governor Gawler proposed a government grant to the Church of England, on the basis that South Australia 'is the most backward of all the colonies … in providing from its public revenues for the means of worshipping that Being to whom we owe our existence and all the blessings we enjoy.' Petitions for and against State aid were developed and were considered by the Legislative Council.

Captain Bagot opposed the grants, stating he would support grants to build schools and for teachers but not for religion. His experience in Ireland showed it could not be done.

The Advocate-General (William Smillie) said there was a great deficiency. The Ministers were ill-paid.

John Morphett moved that a sum be divided between the different sects of professing Christians in proportion to the census returns. This was carried.

Major O'Halloran moved that Jews also receive a proportion after a petition from them was received.

Captain Bagot said that the Jews have as much right to their share as the Christians have although they are wealthy and probably contribute 30 times as much to the revenue as the average colonists.

The grant to Jews was approved.

Governor Robe asked 'Do you mean to propose pagans?'

Captain Bagot said 'Most assuredly. All who contribute.'

Major O'Halloran agreed stating 'I have been in all parts of the world and have seen much of the natives of India, and bear my testimony that more upright and honest men do not exist.'

Concerned colonists formed the League for the Maintenance of Religious Freedom, including Anthony Forster, William Giles, George S. Kingston, William Peacock, and John and Edward Stephens. Its manifesto said:

> 'The evils involved in the principle of State support to religion have been sufficiently obvious to most, if not all of you in the Mother country.' It encouraged 'outward conformity,' corrupted religion by making it formal, and imposed penalties on failure to outward conformity. It 'weakened the State by compelling it to persecute …' Religion was 'purely individual and personal …' A petition was sent to the Queen.

Later Major O'Halloran moved for copies of all Government correspondence with the denominations. This was rejected.

Governor Gawler then laid on the table a Bill providing for 'The building of Places of Worship and making provision for the maintenance of Ministers of Religion.' The League protested.

Mr. Jacob Hagen asked 'Would the Council vote money to assist a number of [Muslims] to build a mosque? … It was one of the inducements held out to early settlers that there should be no State interference with religion and no dominant church.'

He moved to insert the word 'Christian' in the bill.

This was opposed by Major O'Halloran, who said that if the Chinese, Hindus, or New Zealanders came to South Australia, he considered that they would be as fully entitled to their quota as members of the Christian religion. The Jews would be shut out by the motion.

Governor Gawler said that the Council was legislating for the Christian religion not the promotion of Islam.

During a discussion of the amounts, Major O'Halloran said 'The Creator could be worshipped as sincerely in a humble hut as in the proudest cathedral. Sometimes he went to a humble building in his own village and could pray there with as much fervour and zeal as in St John's or St Mary's. It was such places as these humble buildings that he would like to see encouraged.'

Captain Bagot said that the idea of making the sum of money so large as £150 was to create a dominant church.[31] The Bill was carried.

Governor Robe found the constant conflict unpleasant, applied to be relieved of his post, and was given a job in Mauritius.

State aid to religion ended after the 1851 election

After the 1851 election, in which State aid to religion was an important issue, on 29 August 1851, Mr. Gwynne moved the first reading of a Bill 'to continue an ordinance to promote the building of churches and chapels for Christian worship, and to provide for the maintenance of ministers of the Christian religion.' He said, 'it was impossible that any honourable member could dissent from the proposition that it was desirable to promote the Christian religion, or that religion and morals were an unmixed good, and the observance of public worship attended with countless advantages.'

Captain John Hart proposed that the Bill be read for the first time in six months, tantamount to its rejection. He was willing to aid religion in special cases, and rejecting the Bill would prevent much ill-feeling.

George Kingston expressed his regret that the Bill had been introduced when colonists had shown they were all but unanimous against it.

Major Campbell said that the Bill should be thrown out, but it was their duty as legislators to evince support for the Christian religion. Support should be limited to thinly populated districts.

Mr. Finniss said that Christianity was part and parcel of the law of the land. Why should the State be excluded by law from supporting it?

George Hall (who claimed he was 'practically' a voluntarist to get elected) supported the first reading, a community so blessed and favoured by Providence should not refuse to devote a portion of its wealth to the service of God. It was the first step to throwing off allegiance to the King of Kings.

Mr. Baker said that country districts should be supported by State aid. He beseeched members not to throw the Bill out without due discussion, and great injury would be done to the colony if this was noised abroad.

Mr. Dutton said that it would be advisable to reject it without a long discussion.

Mr. Elder said that it was high time for antagonism between the people and the Government to end. Religion could propagate itself without Government aid. Unity between denominations was destroyed by this hateful measure. South Australians would revere the memory of the Dissenters of today.

The Collector of Customs, Mr. Torrens said that the measure would not give predominance to one church; all would benefit. Religion would reclaim the offender and prevent crime, while the strong arm of the law punished.

The Bill was rejected by a majority of three.[32]

On 19 December 1851, Kingston moved in the Legislative Council that grants to all churches come to an end, a radical proposal to separate the church and state.

This was passed, the first such legislation on the Australian continent.[33] This largely ended State aid to religion in South Australia.

Notes

1 Reg Hamilton, Colony, 2010, 91.

2 Reg Hamilton, Colony, 2010, 221, 253, 254.

3 Cityofadelaide.com, Archives, citing Ordinance No.4 of 1840, Clause XII, accessed January 2024.

4 John Keane, *The Life and Death of Democracy* (London: Simon & Schuster UK Ltd, 2009), 520.

5 James Hurtle Fisher and Governor Gawler.

6 sahistoryhub.history.sa.gov.au, Responsible Government, accessed December 2023.

7 Reg Hamilton, Colony, 2010, 224.

8 Reg Hamilton, Colony, 2010, 219.

9 Sean Scalmer, "Containing Contention: A Reinterpretation of Democratic Change and Electoral Reform in the Australian Colonies," *Australian Historical Studies* 42, no. 3 (2011), 352–53.

10 Reg Hamilton, Colony, 2010, 225.

11 Edward Sweetman, *Australian Constitutional Development* (Melbourne: Macmillan & Co Limited in Association with Melbourne University Press, 1925), 310.

12 An Act to Establish a Parliament in South Australia 1853, reserved November 1853 and disallowed.

13 John Blackett, *History of South Australia* (Adelaide: Hussey & Gillingham, 1911), 256–74. This constitutional debate is taken from Blackett, who often summarises rather than quotes the debate. I have paraphrased some of the longer passages to shorten them while retaining their meaning and omitted speakers who simply supported one side or the other.

14 Edward Sweetman, *Australian Constitutional Development* (Melbourne: Macmillan & Co Limited in Association with Melbourne University Press, 1925), 313.

15 A.C.V. Melbourne, *Early Constitutional Development in Australia* (St Lucia: University of Queensland Press 1963), 399–400.

16 Sweetman, *Australian Constitutional Development*, 1925, 313–18.

17 C. Fort, *Electing responsible government: South Australia 1857* (Adelaide: State Electoral Office, 2001); D. Pike, *A Paradise of Dissent: South Australia 1829–1857* (Melbourne: Melbourne University Press, 1967).

18 South Australian Register, 10 December 1855, 1.
19 South Australian Register, 10 December 1855, 4.
20 South Australian Register, 19 December 1855, 4–10
21 South Australian Register, 24 December 1855, 2–3.
22 South Australian Constitution 1856, clause 3.
23 Hamilton, Colony, 2010, 167.
24 Hamilton, Colony, 2010, Chapter 15.
25 Hamilton, Colony, 2010, 8, 216, 220, 224, 225, 226.
26 Hamilton, Colony, 2010, 230–31.
27 Hamilton, Colony, 2010, 230–31.
28 "SA firsts – timeline for South Australian firsts," Parliament South Australia website. https://www.parliament.sa.gov.au/en/About-Parliament/Timelines-for-SA-Firsts, accessed February 2023.
29 John Blackett, *History of South Australia* (Adelaide: Hussey & Gillingham, 1911), 212–18.
30 Russell Smith, *1850, A Very Good Year in the Colony of South Australia* (Sydney: Shakespeare Head Press, 1973), 50.
31 John Blackett, *History of South Australia* (Adelaide: Hussey & Gillingham, 1911, 221–31). This debate is taken from Blackett, who usually summarises rather than quotes the debate. I have paraphrased some of the longer passages to shorten them while retaining their meaning and omitted speakers who simply supported one side or the other.
32 John Blackett, *History of South Australia* (Adelaide: Hussey & Gillingham, 1911), 243–47. This debate is taken from Blackett, who often summarises rather than quotes the debate. I have paraphrased some of the longer passages to shorten them while retaining their meaning and omitted speakers who simply supported one side or the other.
33 These dates, motions, and resolutions are taken from "Votes and Proceedings of the Legislative Council."

Bibliography

Books and articles

Blackett, John. *History of South Australia*. Adelaide: Hussey & Gillingham, 1911.
Fort, C. *Electing Responsible Government: South Australia 1857*, Adelaide: State Electoral Office, 2001.
Hamilton, Reg, Hamilton, Reg. *Colony* Strange Origins of One of the Earliest Modern Democracies. Kent Town, South Australia: Wakefield Press, 2010.
Keane, John. *The Life and Death of Democracy*. London: Simon & Schuster UK Ltd, 2009.
Melbourne, A. C. V. *Early Constitutional Development in Australia*. St Lucia: University of Queensland Press, 1963.
Pike, Douglas. *A Paradise of Dissent: South Australia 1829–1857*. Melbourne: Melbourne University Press, 1967.
Scalmer, Sean. "Containing Contention: A Reinterpretation of Democratic Change and Electoral Reform in the Australian Colonies," *Australian Historical Studies* 42, no. 3 (2011).
Sweetman, Edward. *Australian Constitutional Development*. Melbourne: Macmillan & Co Limited in association with Melbourne University Press, 1925.

Other

Cityofadelaide.com, Ordinance No.4 of 1840, Archives, accessed February 2024.
sahistoryhub.history.sa.gov.au, Responsible Government, accessed December 2023.
"SA firsts –timeline for South Australian firsts." Parliament South Australia website.
  https://www.parliament.sa.gov.au/en/About-Parliament/Timelines-for-SA-Firsts, ac-
  cessed February 2023.
South Australian Register.
SA Ordinance No.4 of 1840.
SA, 'Votes and Proceedings of the Legislative Council'.
An Act to Establish a Parliament in South Australia 1853, reserved November 1853
  and disallowed.

9   The British framework for development of the new constitutions

Abstract

The Australian Constitutions Act 1850 (UK) was a deliberate decision by the Whig Government of Earl Russell to allow constitutions in the form which colonists themselves would develop, and self-government after further agitation and debate in 1852. British election debates and platforms resembled those in the Australian colonies, but the same democratisation did not occur in Britain, where the Chartists were completely defeated. Britain did not experience the European revolutions of 1830 and 1848, and the constant revolutions of France and South America. Britain's Australian colonies shared in this relative stability.

The framework for the Australian colonial debate and new constitutions

Earl Russell were as Prime Minister spoke to Bill, which led to the Australian Constitutions Act 1850.[1] The Act gave the Councils and the governor in each colony the power to implement self-government and extended the New South Wales Constitution of 1842 to the other colonies, with amendments. He examined Britain's history of providing its colonies with elected assemblies and political rights and said that this practice promoted a harmonious feeling between Britain and the colonies:

> It appears to me, that in providing that wherever Englishmen went, they should enjoy English freedom, and have English institutions, they acted justly and wisely. They adopted a course which was calculated to promote a harmonious feeling between the mother country and the colonies ....[2]

While some Australian colonies would become 'independent of England,' this would not happen now:

> But let us make them as far as possible, fit to govern themselves – let us give them, as far as we can, the capacity of ruling their own affairs – let them increase in wealth and population, and whatever may happen, we of this great empire shall have the consolation of saying that we have contributed to the happiness of the world.[3]

DOI: 10.4324/9781003490739-10

Figure 9.1 The Right Hon. Earl Russell, Prime Minister of the United Kingdom
1846–1852. He spoke to the Bill that became the Australia Constitutions
Act 1850

The framework for the development of the constitutions in each colony
was set by the Australian Constitutions Act 1850, which provided that each
colony could elect a Legislative Council under a wide franchise and that the
Council could draft a constitution. Each colony did so.

British limitations on self-government

While the colonies enjoyed self-government, and the local governors acted
on the instructions of ministers responsible to the locally elected legislature
local governors were guided by Royal Instructions which forbade them to
give assent to certain matters such as restrictions on freedom of religion and
the granting of a divorce. Secondly, the UK secretary of state could void colonial legislation by simple Order-in-Council. Thirdly, no law 'repugnant to
the law of England,' such as laws permitting slavery, would be valid. All these

restrictions lessened over the decades.[4] The Colonial Laws Validity Act of 1865 limited repugnancy to specific inconsistency with an imperial Act.[5]

More generally local views increasingly prevailed because of their force and stridency as democracy consolidated.

The Australian debate compared to the UK debate

Even after the Great Reform Act of 1832, the House of Commons represented only a small minority of British men, perhaps one in 5 or 20 per cent of adult males.[6] It was, however, a parliament of free speech, which together with the partly free press, debate during elections and the development of party platforms of policy, provided Britain with a robust but limited democracy in which only men of property could vote.

An example of the wide-ranging British debate is given by the elections 1832–1841 in West Riding, a Yorkshire electorate. The policy issues which dominated the hustings of West Riding in that decade were centred around demands from the working classes for social and political reform[7]:

> Thus, Ellis Cunliffe Lister, MP for Bradford, in his address to electors in the 1837 general election, stated:
>
> I do not recommend you press for universal suffrage; get household suffrage first, and then try what you can get afterwards. You have a right to petition for it, and I will advise you to petition for it again and again, and don't cease because you are not answered at once. Be like the women with the unjust judge: go on petitioning, and I can assure you I will cheerfully present them.

This could be roughly translated as I do not approve of further reform myself, but you, the electorate, are welcome to petition for what you want, and I will present the petitions knowing that they will have little impact upon the Whig government. In summary, the Whigs of the West Riding and nationally were masters of inaction, neither encouraging nor discouraging the burgeoning political reform movements. They were not an entirely negative force but close to it.

Issues discussed in West Riding included the poor law, economic distress of the working classes, votes for all men, the secret ballot, church reform, the Corn Laws and the price of bread, factory reform and industrialisation, Tory paternalism and the young England movement remembering a perhaps fictitious but more caring English social system, social responsibility to the poor, 'Bastille despots,' the problem of increasing Government debt, and the need for increased educational provision and were in many cases not addressed.[8]

A Whig platform in the 1841 contest in Leeds was described by the Whig agent as follows,[9] in particular a Whig would oppose extension of voting rights until there was universal education, then he would support extension:

> In addition to these matters mentioned in your political creed you will, I have no doubt be asked to state publicly:
>
> 1 Will you vote for the abolition of church rates? [Answer: 'As church rates are by Law and a cause of much bitterness, that the remedy is a Law for their abolition – this you might safely say you could vote for.']
> 2 Will you promote any enquiry for cutting off useless pensions and reducing national expenditure? [Answer: 'I have not heard much about pensions, but it would be safe to say that you would try to abolish all forms which did not merit the national honour.']
> 3 Will you consider the reduction of taxation and in what way will you promote it? [Answer: 'This tends to a Property Tax. I should answer this difficult question by saying that I consider all taxes obnoxious and that therefore I should not substitute one tax for another, till I had fully tried those fiscal reforms which if the calculators' purposes were true would not only supersede the necessity of new taxes, but would reduce those already in existence.']
> 4 Will you promote national education? [Answer: 'Yes.']
> 5 Will you object to an extension of the suffrage? [Answer: 'Yes till the national education of the people was established, then I would consider its extension permanent.']
> 6 Are you for shortening the duration of parliaments? [Answer: 'Yes.']

The great Whig Macaulay gave a speech in answer to the Chartists in 1842. He supported the secret ballot but thought that giving all men the vote would expose property owners and the country to disaster, particularly without education of the general working classes[10]:

> Our honest working man has not received such an education as enables him to understand that the utmost distress that he has ever known is prosperity when compared with the distress which he would have to endure if there were a single month of general anarchy and plunder.

Whigs supported abolition of taxes and payments to churches.

However the British Parliament resisted full democratisation until the 20th century, although one in three men could vote for the House of Commons after reforms in 1867.

The Australian colonies were in advance of Britain in developing modern constitutions that reconciled democracy with property rights. Britain did not simply confer democracy on its colonies. It was a local struggle of great difficulty and complexity and the same in Britain itself. We should not however conceal the debt we owe to British political thinking and party platforms which formulated the correct questions and even answers in what Boyle Travers Finniss called the 'advanced' liberalism of Britain.

Why did the Chartists or Chartist style radicals fail in Britain and succeed in Britain's Australian colonies?

Britain had an aristocracy with ancient privileges, and many seats in the House of Commons were controlled by local aristocrats. There was no Australian established nobility or system of hierarchy and privilege as there was, for example, in Canadian Quebec, where Cardinal Richelieu established a colonial feudal aristocracy, under the seigneurial system. Britain had a Constitution of 'time immemorial,' which reflected centuries of political struggle. Britain had established local and varying methods of voting and representation which were tightly controlled by local interests. The Australian colonies did not have such a well-established system of vested interests, except the British Constitution as it applied in the New World.

In Britain the Charter faced real opposition from established interests. At St Peter's fields in Manchester in 1819, a radical meeting calling for votes for all men was attacked and 15 people were killed by a calvary charge in the 'Peterloo massacre' – a reference to the battle of Waterloo. A Chartist petition was not even accepted by parliament in 1848, although violence was avoided. Something had been learned from Peterloo.

In the 1850s more liberal members of each colonial Parliament were close to the Chartists of 1848 in their political positions. The Chartists were eventually a majority in the Parliaments of the three radical colonies not refusing to accept a Chartist petition. There were radicals in the House of Commons but they were heavily outnumbered by Whigs, Liberals and Conservatives who opposed one man one vote.

In 1837, 115 MPs in the British House of Commons called themselves Whigs, 147 Reformers, 42 Radical Reformers, and just 3 Liberals. In 1847, 168 MPs called themselves Liberals (basically free traders), 51 Whigs, 38 Reformers, 22 Repealers, and 21 Radicals. In 1852, 179 MPs called themselves Liberals, 53 Whigs, 51 Reformers, or Radical Reformers, and 12 Repealers. In 1857, most non-Conservative MPs were Liberals, 34 Whigs, 12 radicals, 22 Reformers, and 9 Repealers.

Whigs, Liberals, and Conservatives together blocked one man one vote after 1832 until 1867, when further reforms were introduced which led to perhaps one in three rather than one in five men in Britain having the vote.[11] All men were given the vote in 1918.

The Australian colonies were new societies with less entrenched interests and almost no entrenched voting and similar laws. Attempts to construct a facsimile of the landed interests or men of property of the old country and to sustain their influence by limiting voting to men of property were largely unsuccessful.

The process of adapting the British constitution was a mature, and far more respectful and sensible version of Henry Lawson's impassioned call for reform. Lawson, an alcoholic, sometimes seems to write under the influence of a hangover or the depression he suffered from, but with wonderful effect:

> Sons of the South, awake! arise!
>   Sons of the South, and do.
> Banish from under your bonny skies
> Those old-world errors and wrongs and lies.
> Making a hell in a Paradise
>   That belongs to your sons and you.
>
> Sons of the South, make choice between
>   (Sons of the South, choose true),
> The Land of Morn and the Land of E'en,
> The Old Dead Tree and the Young Tree Green,
> The Land that belongs to the lord and the Queen,
>   And the Land that belongs to you.[12]

Despite attempts, no definition of 'men of property' based on the value of property held was successfully maintained in Australia, except for in the upper houses of parliament, where property qualifications for voting lasted in South Australia until 1973.

French or Spanish Australian colonies – what if?

Australia could have been colonised by other European countries. The French and Dutch explored the coast of Australia. As colonies of France, the Australian colonies would have been subject to a tradition of revolution which began with the French Revolution. In the 19th century this included competing and changing royal houses and changes from monarchy to a republic, revolutions in 1830 and 1848 which overthrew the government, the Paris Commune of 1870, and constitutions and laws which were successively liberal or reactionary, republican or monarchical. The Second Republic was established after the revolution of 1848 (1848–1852), and the Second Empire (1852–1870) was established by Napoleon III in a coup d'état. Under the authoritarian Second Empire, Napoleon III exercised virtually all powers of government.[13] This was the French Government as Australian colonies drafted radically democratic constitutions in the 1850s.

The basic structure of the early liberal democracies established in the Australian colonies in the 1850s can be found in the British constitution amended as demanded by the Chartists. At best the unstable Third Republic (1870–1940), riven as it was by conflicts between republicans and monarchists, could have eventually produced a similar result.[14] France did briefly enact universal suffrage in 1792 and 1848.

The Spanish New World was even more unstable. Argentina had 20 or more revolutions after Napoleon removed the King of Spain in 1802. Squatters and the conservatives did not dominate Australian politics as they did in Latin America. One writer sees British rule as a 'counterweight against the de facto power of the squatters,' without which 'the Latin American outcome seems more probable' meaning 'repression.' Even Argentina lagged behind Australian prosperity.[15]

If Britain, France, Spain, or another European power had not colonised Australia then presumably we would look to other developing countries in our region and elsewhere for how the country might have developed. It would likely not be a first-world developed country if the example they provide can be used as guidance.

The 1850s to the 1930s saw some 50 million Chinese, the same number of Europeans, and 30 million Indians migrate to new lands in search of a better life for themselves and their families.[16]

There were vast movements of people during prehistory, now identified through modern DNA research. In Britain, the colonising power, and in other countries, there were almost complete replacements of peoples in prehistoric times, and then again there were waves of settlers in historical periods.[17] Many European countries have a similar history, as do apparently many modern nation-states in Africa, Asia, and the Americas.

The astonishing remoteness of the Australian continent meant fewer new peoples, but the European voyages of discovery beginning in the late Middle Ages brought the most remote parts of our world into contact with each other and changed that forever.

Notes

1 An account of development of this Act is contained in John Ward, *Earl Grey and the Australian Colonies 1846–1857* (Carlton, Victoria: Melbourne University Press, 1958).

2 8 February 1850, the House of Commons, Hansard Third Series, vol. 108, 549. See Reg Hamilton, *Colony*.

3 House of Commons, Hansard Third Series, vol 108, 567.

4 WG McMinn, *A Constitutional History of Australia* (Melbourne: Oxford University Press, 1979), 79–80

5 McMinn, *A Constitutional History of Australia*, 1979, 79–84.

6 John A. Phillips and Charles Wetherell, "The Great Reform Act of 1832 and the Political Modernisation of England," *The American Historical Review* 100, no. 2 (Apr.1993): 414.

7 Sarah Richardson, "Independence and Deference: A Study of the West Riding Electorate, 1832–1841," PhD thesis, 1995, 29. DX218638_1_0001.tif (whiterose.ac.uk), accessed April 2023

8 Richardson, Independence and Deference: A Study of the West Riding Electorate, 1832–1841, 1995, 35–49.
9 Richardson, Independence and Deference: A Study of the West Riding Electorate, 1832–1841, 1995, 51.
10 Hansard, vol. 63, 3 May 1842. Opposition to universal suffrage (historyhome.co.uk); accessed May 2024.
11 Angus Hawkins, Victorian Political Culture: 'Habits of Heart and Mind' Oxford, Oxford University Press, 2015, Chapters 3, Parliamentary Government and its Critics, 14–21.
12 Henry Lawson, Song of the Republic, 1887.
13 JJ Norwich, *France: A History: From Gaul to de Gaulle* (London: Hachette, 2019), 281–305.
14 Norwich, France: A History: From Gaul to de Gaulle, 2019, 306–37.
15 IW McLean, *Why Australia Prospered: The Shifting Sources of Economic Growth* (Princeton University Press, 2013), 12, 79.
16 M Lake, "Colonial Australia and the Asia-Pacific Region," in *The Cambridge History of Australia*, ed. A Bashford and S Macintyre, vol. 1 (Port Melbourne, Vic.: Cambridge University Press, 2013), 541.
17 D Reich, *Who We Are and How We Got Here* (Oxford: Oxford University Press, 2018); e.g. the Romans, Anglo-Saxons, Vikings, Normans.

Bibliography

Bongiorno, Frank. *Dreamers and Schemers* Collingwood VIC, Australia: La Trobe University Press in conjunction with Black Inc., 2022.

Hamilton, Reg. *Colony: Strange Origins of One of the Earliest Modern Democracies*, Kent Town, Adelaide: Wakefield Press, 2010.

Lake, Marilyn. "Colonial Australia and the Asia-Pacific Region." In *The Cambridge History of Australia*, edited by Alison Bashford and Stuart Macintyre, vol. 1. Port Melbourne, Vic.: Cambridge University Press, 2013.

McLean, Ian W. *Why Australia Prospered: The Shifting Sources of Economic Growth*. Princeton, New Jersey: Princeton University Press, 2013.

McMinn, Winston, G. *A Constitutional History of Australia*. Melbourne: Oxford University Press, 1979.

Melbourne, Alexander C. V. "The Establishment of Responsible Government." In *The Cambridge History of the British Empire*, edited by Ernest Scott, vol. vii, Part I, 274–75. Cambridge: CUP, 1933.

Norwich, John J. *France: A History: From Gaul to de Gaulle*. London, Hachette, 2019.

Phillips, John A., and Charles Wetherell. "The Great Reform Act of 1832 and the Political Modernisation of England." *The American Historical Review* 100 no. 2 (Apr.1993): 414.

Reich, David. *Who We Are and How We Got Here*. Oxford: Oxford University Press, 2018.

Richardson, Sarah. "*Independence and Deference: A Study of the West Riding Electorate, 1832–1841.*" PhD thesis, 1995, 29.

Sarah Richardson, "Independence and Deference: A Study of the West Riding Electorate, 1832–1841," DX218638_1_0001.tif (whiterose.ac.uk), accessed April 2023

Sweetman, Edward. *Australian Constitutional Development.* Melbourne: Macmillan & Co Limited in association with Melbourne University Press, 1925.

Ward, John. *Earl Grey and the Australian Colonies 1846–1857.* Carlton, Victoria. Melbourne University Press, 1958.

Other

Opposition to universal suffrage (historyhome.co.uk); accessed May 2024.

Lawson, Henry. *Song of the Republic.* 1887 https://api.parliament.uk/historic-hansard/index.html, UK Hansard.

10 Conclusion

An assessment of the 1850s constitutional debates

Abstract

The old-fashioned Whig view of William Wentworth, 'Alphabet' Foster, and John Baker of parliament representing all the interests of the colony, property as well as population, substantially the British parliament of the time, was met by colonial liberals who sought a radical new democratic experiment. The new resulting 1850s constitutions and electoral laws were arguably the most Benthamite or Chartist constitutions in the world but with obstructive Legislative Councils. These new liberal democratic parliaments controlled by popular opinion were developed without revolution or civil war but by constitutional argument and democratic mass meetings. They did not collapse under the pressures of governing. Both may be comparatively rare.

Sir Humphrey Appleby:

A minister can do what he likes.

James Hacker:

It's the people's will. I am their leader. I must follow them.

Yes Minister, BBC.

The most Benthamite or Chartist constitutions in the world of the 1850s?

Boyle Travers Finniss, South Australia's first Premier under self-government, said local adoption of 'the advanced liberal principles in the mother country,' meant that 'no man can gain or hold power' unless 'he not only professes but acts in the full determination to use his influence and his power to promote the general advance of the community in wealth by such measures as shall tend to its distribution, not amongst any particular class but amongst those who have raised him to power by their votes, and who, under the present political and commercial systems, are not receiving their just share of the increasing wealth of the State.'[1]

DOI: 10.4324/9781003490739-11

The 1850s debates resulted in what were among the most thoroughly Benthamite or Chartist constitutions in the world of the time, combining individualism with the greatest good for the greatest number:

Many aspects of Australian life can be considered as resulting from the design of the Benthamite polity, with its tendency towards individualism but with a valid role for state action providing conditions for the greatest happiness.[2]

Figure 10.1 Travers Boyle Finniss, first Premier of South Australia

The United States of America was arguably equally or more democratic but for the 'peculiar institution' of slavery, but also always had a less important role for a Benthamite remedial state. Property qualifications for voting were retained in Canada and varied by province. The remarkable democracies of Europe usually had a longer and more difficult path of liberalisation after the failure of the 1848 revolutions, and those of Asia and the rest of the world even longer still.

The Australian liberal constitutions were a rudimentary form of those still operating today over 150 years later.[3] They were seen as a significant achievement by the colonials of the time such as Boyle Travers Finniss.

Walter Bagehot discussed a theory of the British constitution as

a balanced union of three powers. It is said that the monarchical element, the aristocratic element, and the democratic element, have each a share in the supreme sovereignty, and that the assent of all three is necessary to the action of that sovereignty.[4]

The new Australian constitutions had the monarch (Queen and Governors) and the commons, although a far more radically democratic commons than the House of Commons. Colonists found a replacement for the absent aristocracy in property. Legislative Councils were elected with strong property qualifications or nominated, and unequal electorates in the Legislative Assembly gave representation to property, as well as population and simple citizenship. They were a more equal British House of Commons. William Wentworth and other old-fashioned Whigs, or British traditionalists, succeeded in introducing a constitution which balanced the interests of population, property, and the Governor. They supported an old fashioned Whiggery in which parliament ruled but not the Governor or people, approximating the British constitution of the time in the circumstances of the colonies.[5] However they failed to prevent government by the people and democracy. The balance was with the people.

In Britain the 'mixed' or 'balanced' constitution was far less democratic. Even electoral reforms in 1867 led to only one third of men rather than one in five eligible to vote for the House of Commons.

Critics and supporters

Macauley and others were wrong to see democratization as the start of anarchy, lawlessness, and destruction of property (although this was the colonies not Britain). Premier Donaldson, the first Premier under self-government in NSW, was wrong to see democratization as the start of another Great Terror of the French Revolution.[6] The result was the reverse. Indeed a lack of democratization may have seen the South American result, that of continuing destructive revolutionary upheavals and the continued influence of the large landowners, the 'squatters,' as George Kingston and others warned. The vision of the squatters at one stage was continuing transportation of convicts for example and a very different society and economy.

Were James Macarthur (and arguably Wentworth) wrong to say that democratization would lead to Americanism and republicanism? The Queen visited Australia and New Zealand in 1954, 100 years later as part of a tour of the Commonwealth, and Canada later in 1957. Her reception could not have been more enthusiastic. A referendum in 1999 to make Australia a republic was defeated.[7] Australia is not a republic in 2024. The Crown has direct links to the States.[8] The United States has replaced Britain as the main cultural and defence influence. American films, politics, and culture have 'colonized the world' including Australia.

Nevertheless at the Grand National Banquet held on 17 July 1856 to commemorate the advent of responsible government, Sir William Bland was chairman and said that the Australia Constitution Act 1850 ranked with 'those splendid, those wise measures: the Emancipation Bill, the Abolition of Slavery, the Repeal of the Corn Laws, and the inauguration of Free Trade … the epic poetry of history.'[9] The Act did have the effect Earl Russell called for in speaking to it in Parliament, namely the continuation of close and friendly relations, even helping some form of continuing political and cultural 'Anglosphere' between the United States, Britain, Australia, Canada, and New Zealand, between Britain and its English speaking former colonies.[10]

Serle said of the Victorian constitution 'there was little in the debates of these founding fathers to set before schoolchildren with patriotic pride. The general intellectual level was abysmal; nobody remotely approached the level of a Wentworth.'[11]

Wentworth was a key leader of self-government. Because of Wentworth there was a mechanism of extreme last resort to resolve disputes between the houses in NSW, namely 'swamping' the upper house with new appointments, just as the House of Lords could be swamped and nearly was after rejecting the Reform Bill 1831. In Victoria and South Australia there was no mechanism and disputes between the houses were arguably more difficult to resolve.

Blackett said of the radical South Australian debate 'The members rose to the occasion. The debate was a lofty and statesmanlike one. The members felt that they were making history – that they had arrived at a critical time in the building up of the Commonwealth. This Council will ever have historical value.'[12] They made decisions which were durable, namely the introduction of the most radical liberal democratic constitution.

The Australian colonies had no organised political parties and partly anticipated A.C. Grayling's suggestion that Government must not be simply majority rule but act in the interests of all by transcending politics for the public interest. The chaotic practice of colonial self-government somewhat discredits the suggestion. The new constitutions did not define the nature and extent and limits of the powers of all the institutions as he suggested.[13] That was to be painfully worked out.

Donald Horne spoke of a lucky country run by second-rate individuals using derivative ideas.[14] William Wentworth and Catherine Helen Spence had unquenchable energy and imagination and were not simply derivative. The democratic results were remarkable for the time. Democracy could have been delayed as it was in Canada and Britain. The combination of loyalist British traditions and an experimental radical Chartism was durable and survived great friction between property and mass politics.

As the Victorian Surveyor-General said in 1853 Britain tried and failed to make acceptable constitutions and now we 'have no precedents, no traditions, no former practice to lead us.'[15] The Victorian Collector of Customs said that there were many colonies but 'the present is almost the only case in which a Colony has been, almost without restriction, called upon to propound for itself … its wishes and its views.' Self-government was 'an experiment.'[16]

Figure 10.2 Hon. John Baker, led the movement to restrict democracy in South Australia

The 1837 Canadian rebellions did not result in an equivalent to the Australian Constitutions Act 1850 (UK) in which Canadians drafted their own constitutions with votes for all men and the secret ballot. Canada was a precedent for self-government with traditional British property qualifications for voting.[17]

Nor was the achievement of local democracy just accidental or inglorious.[18] Robert Lowe lowered the voting requirements in the Australia Constitutions Act 1850 by deceit, but without liberal campaigns including to get him elected and promoting liberalization, democracy would have been restricted more by William Wentworth, JLFV ('alphabet') Foster, John Baker, and others who showed considerable resistance to democracy and were determined and able leaders. Perhaps the 1850 Act franchise could not have been made more restrictive; perhaps Wentworth and others could have tried. Without liberalizing campaigns there would have been no Australian Constitutions Act 1850. Aboriginal people were critics as well as sometimes conditional supporters. A Kaurna address in Adelaide to Governor Gawler when he left in 1841 is an early statement of Aboriginal objectives of respectful treatment, rations, land, and teaching of children:

> Us, the chest beats at his absence. Our commander, he did sit; on his side we did sit. For us he did contend. He us did hide from the white men who insulted. Lament we at his absence. He at us well did look. Our father he did sit; regarding food, meat, clothing. Food, clothing, he did give. Land for food he gave us back. Schoolhouse he for the children of us did build. Words to learn as white children.[19]

The net effect of such interactions over generations in countless places is 'complex' and 'complicated' and some were far less benign.[20]

In 2014 Noel Pearson wrote that

> Our nation is in three parts. There is our ancient heritage, written in the continent and the original culture painted on its land and seascapes. There is our British inheritance, the structures of government and society transported from the United Kingdom fixing its foundations in the ancient soil. There is our multicultural achievement: a triumph of immigration that brought together the gifts of peoples and cultures from all over the globe – forming one indissoluble commonwealth.[21]

A cornucopia of bad ideas

The world was and is a cornucopia of bad ideas and bad governance. The 20th-century evils of totalitarian fascism and communism were a comprehensive rejection of democracy and were on most counts responsible for the greatest number of government caused deaths in history.[22] They had a precursor in the Great Terror of the French Revolution (1789–1799) at the end of the 18th century and much later revolutionary and ultra-nationalist belligerent ranting in Europe. A small group of liberal democracies, including the United States, Britain, France, Canada, Australia, New Zealand, the Netherlands, the Scandinavian countries, and other European powers, held out against those terrible evils between the great wars (1919–1939).

The 1850s Australian democracy debates are amongst the precursors of the liberal and social democratic thinking of that embattled group of liberal democracies.

The 1850s parliamentarians took the best from the British and Chartist models

It was difficult to experiment and establish a constitution which would survive in each turbulent colony with the 'spirit of democracy abroad' and the need for mass democratic participation to 'constrain' violence and disorder. There was no exact precedent; the successful democracy of the United States started with a violent revolution.

Instead of a revolution the Legislative Councils took the British constitution and the Chartists, but also other models, and turned them into workable documents that reconciled parliaments to popular opinion and the new world of mass political debate.

Legislative Councils sought self-government but not an independent country and accepted with reservations a continuing British role. Legislative Council attempts to restrict Britain's power to disallow local legislation were rejected by Britain.

Parliamentarians of the 1850s discarded less workable British practices such as seven-year terms of parliament. Even the upper house property qualifications excluded far less than the 80 per cent of adult men excluded from voting for the House of Commons.

It was a new world.

Stability from a British framework

Britain was not rejected. The Crown was not rejected. Property rights were not rejected except for land reform. A limited constitutional monarchy and successful market economy were the result. It was self-government of local affairs adopting British forms and stability. Foreign affairs were left with Britain. This had not been open to the Americans.

Strong support for British institutions and liberalism amongst the general population was essential to this success. Stable parliamentary debate was the tribal system supported by mostly British colonists, supplemented by the usual petitions, riots, 'monster meetings,' inflammatory newspapers and books and later political parties. The role of parliament in British culture was entrenched. The rebel Jack Cade, who came out of Kent in 1450 to challenge maladministration, was made by Shakespeare to declare 'burn all the records of the realm: my mouth shall be the parliament of England.' He was a grandiose and ridiculous figure of presumption.[23]

Colonial advanced liberalism was within the scope of respectable or semi-respectable British political thought, and it did not lurch into the French Revolution great terror or anything approaching it. The French revolutionaries closed the churches, executed the monarch, imprisoned and killed large numbers without due process, and set up a cult of reason to replace Christianity. They even renamed the months of the year.

Unlike France ('l'Hexagone, or 'The Hexagon' in shape although it borders eight countries) and the other European powers, who were repeatedly threatened and invaded, the colonies had a benign geopolitical environment of no external threats because of remoteness, although they had geopolitical concerns. They set up militias in each colony in response to an imaginary Russian threat made apparent by the Crimean War in the 1850s and Alfred Deakin expressed concern about French and German colonial incursions into the Pacific at the Imperial Conference in 1887.

The Legislative Council members were able to address fundamental democratization and practical issues of legislative powers and self-government without questioning the sovereignty of Westminster. The debates assumed Westminster sovereignty and the Australian Constitutions Act 1850.

Defence and foreign affairs controlled by the British were apparently satisfactory or needed, and the sense of Australian national identity was less than it became later in the century. Indeed an ordinary British patriotism was expressed by local leaders while commemorating colony events.

Vulnerable developing colonies

The Australian colonies in the 1850s were what we would now describe as 'developing' or 'third world,' with a standard of living well below what we enjoy today. Real colonial per capita GDP increased between four and six times between 1861 and 1991.[24]

Ordinary people benefited from the market economy through employment and good wages, largely 'riding on the sheep's back,' although many other industries developed. The achievements of colonial liberals included land reform, consolidation of democracy, a range of other reforms such as Torrens title and beginning in the 1890s the development of the modern safety net of welfare, labour laws, health, and education systems. This addressed the needs of the poor and vulnerable, those left behind the general prosperity, later called a 'fair go.' This introduced a common citizenship.

An ameliorative liberalism developed in which parliaments addressed problems experienced by ordinary people. Voting rights became indeed as the Chartists said 'a knife and fork question.' Occasional violence did not develop into a civil war.

These were mature legislative exercises in balancing economic sustainability and demonstrated actual need and rested on a strong and productive market economy. Vast and divisive debates took place on these and other policy problems[25] and still occur today.

The less democratic upper houses obstructed land reform which was the result of 'a popular campaign of four years and by political pressure' rather than 'the deliberate wisdom of the parliament' in NSW.[26] It took actual swamping of the NSW upper house and several crises in Victoria for the legislation to pass. Then squatters used dummies to bid for their own land and avoid redistribution in NSW, although crown lands were successfully distributed, at the expense of local Aboriginal people. Nevertheless squatters were pushed to the less desirable outer lands in each colony,[27] and land was reallocated without serious conflict which threatened the small democracies; rather the democracies provided a means of resolving the conflicts.[28]

There was some corruption with pastoralists in Victoria maintaining a secret fund during the 1860s used to bribe members of the Legislative Assembly, for example, and some corruption over railway line allocation. Pastoralists were dominant in the Victorian Legislative Council, a third of the Legislative Assembly in NSW in 1860 and a fifth as late at 1880, and in South Australia a peak of one quarter in 1865 'although they did not vote as a block.'[29]

Land use enabled Australia to 'ride on the sheep's back' and prosper and the influence of the squatters declined.[30]

The upper houses would be more defensible if they had been more representative. At present different voting systems in the lower and upper houses in the four States with upper houses (NSW, Victoria, Western Australia, Tasmania) often produce different majorities to the lower house which are nonetheless defensible as democratic. The upper houses enable the arrogance of power to be tempered, and the fundamental question of most Government legislation to be faced: 'who wins, who loses.' Then it can be transparently confronted and openly debated.

Constitutions are not just a set of legal rules. Good governance was one result of inter-related factors such as 'abundant natural resources,' an educated workforce, and 'an institutional framework that did not impede the emergence and flourishing of risk-taking and profit-seeking enterprise – and that was capable of peaceful adaptation when it threatened to choke off prosperity; and a cultural context, or set of social norms, necessary to the maintenance of good governance.'[31]

Australian colonies left alone to fend for themselves as Spain's South American colonies were after Napoleon removed the Spanish monarch in 1808 might for the purposes of argument have experienced similar rule by the landowners and revolutionary upheavals and resulting poverty. There would have been no Australia Constitutions Act 1850. The squatters would at least have been in a stronger position, although British settlers had a culture of parliament rather than Spanish autocracy.

In that case the squatters and large landowners, and not democrats, would control the government into the 20th century to a greater extent and use it to enrich and protect themselves. However this remote possibility was removed by the countervailing power of British rule in the view of at least one writer.[32] The influence of the squatters dissipated without violence.

Contemporary constitutions

The 1850s constitutions were as already noted democratized further over the next 150 years. The platform of the Charter, so important to the 1850s debates and after, has been implemented (and expanded to include women) except for annual elections and the Australian Senate, where electorates are far from equal but supported in a States' House. Given the general ideals of democracy, electoral systems are under constant review with a view to improvement. Preferential voting was introduced in 1918 and compulsory voting in 1924.

The decision of Legislative Councils to include Aboriginal and Chinese people in voting rights was a remarkable thing for the world of the 1850s when even basic democratic rights for all men were controversial and difficult decisions and only 20 per cent of men in Britain had the vote. Few women in the world would have had the vote exercised by 70 Aboriginal women and men at Point McLeay in South Australia in 1896.[33] Aboriginal people were excluded from voting federally in 1902, which was overturned in 1962, although some State voting rights were preserved by Section 41 of the Constitution.

There is now some limited recognition of Aboriginal and Torres Strait islander people in State constitutions by legislated amendment not referenda.[34] In 1999 a proposal to include a preamble in the Australian constitution recognizing Aboriginal and Torres Strait islander people was heavily defeated in a federal referendum together with an attempt to make Australia a republic.[35] In 2023 a referendum proposal to include an Aboriginal and Torres Strait 'voice' in the Australian constitution was heavily defeated by the same margin.[36]

Aboriginal and Torres Strait traditional land title was discovered in the High Court Mabo decision in 1992 to have always existed.[37]

The wider significance of the 1850s debates

The 1850s debates provide an outline of how the essential elements of modern liberal democracies providing for mass political participation can be put forward and justified over the opposition of men of tradition and property in what were very traditional although turbulent times.

There was no actual precedent from other British colonies that could be simply adopted. It was a trial or experiment although adopted from the advanced liberal thinking that had become part of the British political spectrum.

Then the small democracies survived instability as mass participation self-government consolidated, itself almost unprecedented.

The transition could not have been successful without strong support for liberalism and parliamentary representation amongst the colonists. There were no competing ideologies beyond a traditional and old-fashioned Whiggery, which was in any event about modest concession to popular demands (for example with the 1832 Reform Act which restructured the House of Commons electorates), was not violent, and had the same tradition of parliamentary representation. The losing Whigs, if they did in fact lose, did not resort to squatter armies. The colonies were not simply looted by the new rulers. The squatters did not dominate or overwhelm the new democracies such as to threaten their path to modern economies.

This was both a democratic liberal and a Whig revolution, at a time when Whigs were becoming liberals. The final resolution of the conflict between property and votes for all men was left for democracy in the 20th century. It is odd to think of a Whig shadow constitution operating in South Australia until reform of the Legislative Council in 1973. The colonists clung to the old world even as it was slipping away, but proportionality, limited ambition and government are underrated.

Freedom broadening slowly down – Tennyson and Henry Lawson

The 1850s constitution debates left the Australian colonies and Australia as a country where votes for women could be introduced in South Australia as a simple two-page amendment in 1895, an example of freedom slowly broadening down:

> A land of government,
> A land of just and old renown,
> Where Freedom slowly broadens down
> From precedent to precedent[38]

But Britain's Australian colonies also (like Britain) had occasionally bitter radicalism and incendiary language, although it is arguable that there was never a real possibility of civil war. There was a 'black line' in 1830 in Tasmania in response to a 'virtual state of war' over land. Armed militias confronted the government at Eureka in 1853 over miner's licences, and during the 1891 shearer's strike over wages and trade union recognition.[39]

The bitter and failed shearer's strike came at a time of terrible poverty resulting from drought and recession after a long boom. The strike was defended by the poet Henry Lawson, who wrote[40]

> Our parents toil'd to make a home –
> Hard grubbin 'twas an' clearin' –
> They wasn't crowded much with lords
> When they was pioneering.
> But now that we have made the land
> A garden full of promise,
> Old Greed must crook 'is dirty hand
> And come ter take it from us.

The strikers were defeated without a civil war. This led to the formation of a new Australian Labor Party to represent workers in politics. Together with the Liberal Party of Australia and National parties and others, they now pursue 'knife and fork' issues and are harshly reviewed by an unforgiving electorate.

The genius of the 1850s debates in requiring parliaments responsive to the popular will meant that blood never did 'stain the wattle' in a civil war, Henry Lawson's terrible warning.

Notes

1 Boyle Travers Finniss, *The Constitutional History of South Australia during Twenty-One Years, from the Foundation of the Settlement in 1836 to the Inauguration of Responsible Government in 1857* (W.C. Rigby, 1886), 251, 259.
2 David Llewellyn, "Bentham and Australia," *Revue d'études benthamiennes* (2021): 52. DOI: 10.4000/etudes-benthamiennes.8517.
3 John Waugh, "Framing the First Victorian Constitution, 1853-5," *Monash University Law Review* 23, no. 2 (1997): 21, 331–32.
4 Walter Bagehot, *The English Constitution*, 2nd ed. (Oxford: Oxford University Press, 1963).
5 See for example Angus Hawkins, Victorian Political Culture: 'Habits of Heart and Mind' Oxford: Oxford University Press, 2015, Chapters 3,7,8
6 Wentworth and Donaldson were no doubt exaggerating, even slandering, to achieve their goals of less democracy.
7 Australia had a referendum in 1999 on whether to become a republic. The proposal was rejected 54.87 per cent to 45.13 per cent.
8 The Australia Act 1986 removed British legislative powers but the Australian States still have a direct link to the British Crown. Australia retains strong cultural and political affinities with the United Kingdom and Ireland, the source of most of our population.
9 Edward Sweetman, *Australian Constitutional Development* (Macmillan & Co Limited in association with Melbourne University Press, 1925), 299.
10 An 'Anglosphere' of the United States, United Kingdom, Canada, Australia, and New Zealand is operative in the 'Five Eyes' and 'AUKUS' defence arrangements and elsewhere.
11 Geoffrey Serle, *The Golden Age* (Carlton Vic.: Melbourne University Press, 1977), 339.
12 John Blackett, *History of South Australia* (Adelaide: Hussey & Gillingham, 1911), 256.
13 A.C. Grayling, *The Good State* (London: Oneworld Publications, 2020), 166–67.
14 Donald Horne, *The Lucky Country* (Camberwell, Victoria: Penguin, 1964), introduction to 6th edition.
15 GHF Webb, *Debate in the Legislative Council of the Colony of Victoria on the Second Reading of the New Constitution Bill*, Caleb Turner, Melbourne, 1854, 91–93.
16 Webb, *Debate in the Legislative Council of the Colony of Victoria on the Second Reading of the New Constitution Bill*, 1854, 120–33.
17 Although Nova Scotia had votes for all men aged 21 1854–1863 excluding 'Indians': Elections Canada, Chapter 1 – A History of the Vote in Canada. Canada today is a prosperous, confident, and well-regarded democracy.
18 S Scalmer, "Containing Contention: A Reinterpretation of Democratic Change and Electoral Reform in the Australian Colonies," *Australian Historical Studies* 42, no. 3 (2011): 337–56: 'Dominant interpretations are based on selective surveys of particular colonies; they either elevate the gold diggings or else cynically claim that democratisation was mostly accidental or inglorious. This paper encompasses a survey of the three major colonies. It argues that widespread collective action was a spur to political change, and that electoral reforms were introduced to contain future contention.'
19 Reg Hamilton, *Colony*, 141.

20 Megan Davis, Correspondence, *Quarterly Essay 55, Noel Pearson, A Rightful Place* (Black Inc, September 2014). Kindle edition.

21 Noel Pearson, Symbolic indigenous recognition for all of us, 2 June 2018, Cape York Institute, Media Articles, Our Agenda, Symbolic indigenous recognition for all of us – Noel Pearson – Cape York Partnership, accessed January 2024.

22 Daniel Kopel, reason.com, accessed January 2024.

23 Henry IV, Part II, Act IV, Scene 7.

24 Paul A. Cashin, "Real GDP in the Seven Colonies of Australasia 1861–1991," *Review of Income and Wealth Series* 41, no. 1 (March 1995). Yale University, Table 4, p.28. It varies by colony between a 4 to over 6 times increase. 19.pdf (roiw.org), accessed April 2023.

25 For example, the passage of Victorian wages boards in 1896 was a long and difficult process of negotiation with the less supportive upper house concerned about the effect of the Bill on industry. Three federal governments fell during the passage of the Commonwealth Conciliation and Arbitration Act 1904 and regular crises occurred over amendments to that Act for the rest of the century, for example the defeat of the Bruce Government in 1928, when the Prime Minister, Melbourne Stanley Bruce, lost government and his seat over a radical amendment to that Act.

26 Stephen H. Roberts, *History of Australian Land Settlement* (Macmillan, 1968), 236.

27 Roberts, *History of Australian Land Settlement*, 1968, 302.

28 IW. McLean, Why Australia Prospered: The Shifting Sources of Economic Growth (Princeton University Press, 2013), 99.

29 Frank Bongiorno, *Dreamers and Schemers* (Latrobe University Press, 2022), 55–56, 61.

30 Stephen H. Roberts, *History of Australian Land Settlement* (Macmillan, 1968), 227–300.

31 IW. McLean, *Why Australia Prospered: The Shifting Sources of Economic Growth* (Princeton University Press, 2013), 249.

32 IW. McLean, *Why Australia Prospered: The Shifting Sources of Economic Growth* (Princeton University Press, 2013), 79.

33 Australian Electoral Commission, History of the Indigenous Vote, Electoral milestones for Indigenous Australians – Australian Electoral Commission (aec.gov.au), accessed November 2023. This is something I pointed out in my paper of 31 October 2022, which contained some of these debates.

34 For example, Section 1A of the Constitution Act 1975 (Vic) recognises Aboriginal people of Victoria as the original custodians of the land on which the colony of Victoria was established.

35 Preamble defeated 60.66 per cent to 39.34. Republic defeated 54.87 to 45.13 per cent. No state gave a majority to either proposal, noting a successful federal referendum requires both a majority of votes and a majority of States to vote yes.

36 Defeated 60.1 per cent to 39.9. No state gave a majority to the proposal.

37 Mabo and others v. Queensland (No. 2) [1992] HCA 23; (1992) 175 CLR 1 F.C. 92/014 (3 June 1992) Mabo v. Queensland (No. 1) (1988) 166 CLR 186 F.C. 88/062.

38 Alfred Lord Tennyson, You ask me, why, tho' ill at ease.

39 My distant relative by marriage, James Mansfield Niall, helped organize the 1891 shearers' strike for the pastoralists in Queensland as part of the Central Executive appointed to run the strike. He was working on the sheep yards about five miles from the homestead of his station near Barcaldine and was collected by a four in hand, with his horses in it, driven by four other graziers who had already packed his clothes. They took him to Barcaldine to attend a Pastoralists' Association meeting where his work began. Elsie Richie, ed., For the Love of the Land, The History of the Cudmore Family, Privately Printed 2000, Chapter 13, 'My experiences in the Shearers Strike.' By James Mansfield Niall, 297.

40 Henry Lawson, Freedom on the Wallaby, 1891.

Bibliography

Books and articles

Bagehot, Walter. *The English Constitution*, 2nd ed. Oxford: Oxford University Press, 1963 (reprint).

Blackett, John. *History of South Australia*. Adelaide: Hussey & Gillingham, 1911.

Cashin, Paul A. "Real GDP in the Seven Colonies of Australasia 1861–1991." *Review of Income and Wealth Series* 41, no 1 (March 1995),28 Accessed April 2023.

Craven, Greg. *The Founding Fathers: Constitutional Kings or Colonial Knaves*, Papers on Parliament No. 21, December 1993.

Davis, Megan. Correspondence, *Quarterly Essay 55, A Rightful Place*, Noel Pearson. Collingwood Vic: Black Inc, 2014. Kindle edition.

Elections Canada, Chapter 1 – A History of the Vote in Canada., https://www.elections.ca/content.aspx?section=res&dir=his&document=index&lang=e

Finniss, Boyle Travers. *The Constitutional History of South Australia during Twenty-One Years, from the Foundation of the Settlement in 1836 to the Inauguration of Responsible Government in 1857*, W.C. Rigby, 1886.

Gollan, Robin. *Radical and Working Class Politics*. Melbourne: Melbourne University Press, , 1960.

Grayling, Anthony.C. *The Good State*, 166–67.London: Oneworld Publications, 2020.

Horne, Donald. *The Lucky Country*. Camberwell, Victoria: Penguin, 1964.

Llewellyn, David. "Bentham and Australia." *Revue d'études benthamiennes* 19 (2021). DOI: 10.4000/etudes-benthamiennes.8517.

McLean, Ian W. *Why Australia Prospered: The Shifting Sources of Economic Growth*, 79. Princeton, New Jersey: Princeton University Press, 2013.

Macquarie Concise Dictionary, 166, 5th ed. Sydney: Macquarie Dictionary Publishers Pty Ltd, 1999.

Richie, ElsieElsie, ed. "Chapter 13, 'My experiences in the Shearers Strike.' By James Mansfield Niall." In *For the Love of the Land, the History of the Cudmore Family*, Privately Printed, 2000.

Roberts, Stephen H. *History of Australian Land Settlement*. Melbourne: Macmillan, 1968.

Scalmer Sean. "Containing Contention: A Reinterpretation of Democratic Change and Electoral Reform in the Australian colonies." *Australian Historical Studies* 42, no. 3 (2011).

Serle, Geoffrey. *The Golden Age*. Carlton Vic.: Melbourne University Press, 1977.

Sweetman, Edward. *Australian Constitutional Development*. Carlton Vic.: Macmillan & Co Limited in association with Melbourne University Press, 1925.

Waugh, John. "Framing the First Victorian Constitution, 1853–5." *Monash University Law Review* 23, no. 2. (1997): 21.

Webb, George, HF. *Debate in the Legislative Council of the Colony of Victoria on the Second Reading of the New Constitution Bill*, Caleb Turner, Melbourne.

Other

The Constitution Act 1975 (Vic).

The Australia Act 1986 (Cth.).

Mabo and others v. Queensland (No. 2) [1992] HCA 23; (1992) 175 CLR 1 F.C. 92/014 (3 June 1992).

Mabo v. Queensland (No. 1) (1988) 166 CLR 186 F.C. 88/062.

Kopel, Daniel. reason.com, accessed January 2024.

Pearson, Noel. Symbolic indigenous recognition for all of us, 2 June 2018, Cape York Institute, Media Articles, Our Agenda, Symbolic indigenous recognition for all of us – Noel Pearson – Cape York Partnership, accessed January 2024.

Shakespeare, William. Henry IV Part II.

Lawson, Henry. Freedom on the Wallaby, 1891.

Tennyson, Alfred Lord. You ask me, why, tho' ill at ease.

Appendix
A note on sources

There is no one full record of the debates in the Australian colonial parliaments which led to the constitutions and electoral laws of the 1850s.

The debates or summaries of them in the most radical colony, South Australia, can be found in the South Australian newspapers and records of resolutions of Parliament and similar records, and in John Blackett, History of South Australia, 1911. I have directly quoted much of Blackett and summarised some of it.

There are written compendiums of the debates in Victoria[1] and New South Wales[2] compiled in the 19th century, but they are not the full debates. Hansard records the debates in 1857 which gave all men the vote in Victoria,[3] but there is no equivalent Hansard for New South Wales in 1858.[4] Reports of the debates there must be sought in newspaper reports and, for example, those relating to NSW are not direct reports of what was said, but summaries as in the report of Mr. Campbell in 1858:

> He was also in favour of vote by ballot, as proposed in the bill, because he believed it was the safest protection they could afford the poor against the intimidation of the rich.[5]

The speeches were part of the political process in each colony. Sometimes they were part of a process of testing the house or negotiation to gain support. For example in South Australia, Mr. Baker, a conservative, withdrew his proposal for a literacy test for voting after it was not supported by the Council.

The speeches reflected the different opinions, which can broadly be described as Whig and Liberal, or democratic and less democratic, in each colony, whether through informal canvassing or more formal platforms as outlined. Those elected on a platform of for example democracy would largely reflect those views, in the knowledge that another election would be lost if the platform was not promoted. Nominees were less restrained by public opinion although they could be dismissed for unpopularity.

The speeches were often printed in the local colony newspapers, were read with interest, and influenced public opinion. They were an essential part of the political process in each colony which led to one man, one vote, and the secret ballot.

Notes

1 Debate in the Legislative Council of the Colony of Victoria on the Second Reading of the New Constitution Bill, George H.F. Webb, Melbourne, Caleb Turner, 1854. This can be accessed online at the State Library of Victoria.
2 New South Wales constitution bill; The Speeches, in the Legislative Council of New South Wales, on the second reading of the bill for framing a new constitution for the colony, edited by Edward Kennedy Silvester. This can be accessed online at the State Library of New South Wales.
3 Electoral Act 1857 (Vic).
4 Electoral Reform Act 1858 (NSW).
5 *Sydney Morning Herald*, 7 May 1858, pp. 3–4.

Index

For Product Safety Concerns and Information please contact our EU
representative GPSR@taylorandfrancis.com
Taylor & Francis Verlag GmbH, Kaufingerstraße 24, 80331 München, Germany

www.ingramcontent.com/pod-product-compliance
Lightning Source LLC
Chambersburg PA
CBHW061749270326
41928CB00011B/2428